D0123874

ART RESTORATION

A Guide to the Care
and Preservation of
Works of Art

by
FRANCIS KELLY

McGRAW-HILL BOOK COMPANY
New York: St. Louis: San Francisco

To
MY WIFE GAIL
and our sons
SEAN, DUFF AND JESSE

First published in the United States by
McGraw-Hill Book Company, a subsidiary
of McGraw-Hill, Inc., 1972

SBN: 07-033890-6
Library of Congress Catalog Card Number: 72-177591

First Edition

*Set in Imprint by C. E. Dawkins (Typesetters) Limited, S.E.1
and printed in Great Britain
by Redwood Press Limited, Wiltshire
for David & Charles (Publishers) Limited
South Devon House Newton Abbot Devon*

CONTENTS

LIST OF PLATES

Photographs not acknowledged above are from the author's collection.

PREFACE

This book is written in answer to the many questions about restoration work voiced by artists, collectors, student restorers, dealers, museum curators, and historians, framers, and gallery employees: the professional restorer will be, presumably, already familiar with most of its basic information. It aims to describe the ethics, problems and contributions of the restoring profession, and should also interest those many members of the general public who are interested in paintings and their preservation.

In Chapters VI to IX on Painting Examination, Consolidation and Repair, Cleaning Paintings, and Retouching and Revarnishing, I have tried to follow the logical sequence of restoration procedures to which a painting is subjected after its arrival in the restorer's studio. In Chapter VI on Painting Examination, for example, a particular condition and its probable cause may be described while the method of treatment is subsequently dealt with in a later chapter.

My experience as a painter/etcher has greatly influenced my particular viewpoint in describing the various methods of art restoration. The artist must be aware of his responsibility in providing sound structures and techniques for his creative work. Those who deal in or collect art must learn to recognize signs of deterioration and to assume the obligation of maintenance and preservation of works in their possession.

The years I spent involved with the restoration profession led me to some conclusions about this absorbing field in which the more one learns the more one realizes how much there is still to learn. I have developed a profound respect for the work of the restoring profession and for the dedicated restorer. I have gained an added appreciation of the important role the restorer can play in the future preservation of contemporary art. I feel strongly that the curriculum of fine art institutes should include a course on the introduction to restoring methods and potentialities.

The interest aroused among the general public by the restoration of works of art following the Florence flood disaster has unfortunately not been stimulated, because there is only a limited number of books on the subject of restoration. I hope that this book will help to fill the gap and nurture this interest. No one can be taught restoring by merely reading a book, but perhaps it can act as an incentive for acquiring further knowledge and appreciation of a most worthy profession.

It is my hope that this book will inspire and encourage those interested in the subject of restoration, which is so vital to the art we cherish.

CHAPTER I

CARE OF PAINTINGS AND PRINTS

Introduction

Every work starts off on the progressive path to destruction from the moment it is created. The artist can only hope to delay this time for as long as possible by the judicious choice of materials and their application with a sound technique. When the picture passes from the artist's hands, he can only pray that it will be well looked after. If he is fortunate and the painting survives accident it will be many years before it is in need of a restorer's attention. Even so, it cannot be made to last forever, but with careful restoration and preservation it may continue to please succeeding generations when many of its contemporaries have crumbled to dust.

The subject of restoration holds a fascination for anyone interested in art. In order to maintain and preserve our cultural heritage, the cooperation of every individual involved in the world of art is necessary. The artist should be aware of the permanence of his materials and techniques, and the collector should learn to recognize signs of deterioration in order to assure the proper care and safety of works in his possession.

Paintings have been left stored in unsuitable places, resulting in tragic consequences. In one instance during World War II a valuable panel painting was wrapped and hidden in a hot, dry recess of a hotel kitchen. Although the painting could have been inspected periodically the owner neglected to do this. When the painting was removed from its hiding place and unwrapped at the end of the war the owner was horrified to find that the paint had become detached and lay in a heap of broken particles at the bottom of the stripped panel.

A painting may pass through many hands and survive for centuries if it is correctly cared for. Owners of paintings generally assume that their investment is secure from the time of purchase. They often fail to recognize their continuing responsibility for maintaining the pictures. Neglect can be as devastating to a painting as a poor environment. Failure of the collector to observe and understand the processes of deterioration can lead to a shortened existence for a work of art. Unless signs of deterioration are noted and corrected the painting's future will be in jeopardy and its value will depreciate. It is only through trained observation that less obvious defects can be discovered.

We all look at paintings in different ways. The layman views a painting with perhaps the greatest detachment, usually basing his assessment on the old cliché 'I don't know much about art, but I know what I like.' In some ways this is what we all do, no matter how knowledgeable we are about art. The critic views with some preoccupation. His thoughts are concerned with writing erudite comments or witty reactions. Historians look for clues to periods and events through dress or significant detail. Artists view with an appraisal of the technique and the application of paint. The restorer will inspect a picture at close range, looking for signs of deterioration. He will scrutinize the painting in a nose-to-canvas position for previous damages and overpaint. The future survival of many works may depend upon his expertise.

The Ethics and Responsibilities of the Restorer

The restorer's knowledge and skill are instrumental in deterring rapid deterioration and extending the life span of a picture. A skilled restorer can increase the visual appreciation of a painting and its sales value.

There are, of course, certain limitations to the accomplishments of even the most expert restorer. He is unable, for example, to revive the colour of the paint itself if it has been affected. He cannot truly replace original paint that has been lost, but he can, with the utmost regard for the artist's intent, repaint the missing areas in a manner almost identical in technique and style.

The restorer must assess the extent of possible damage which may not be readily visible before he undertakes the cleaning of a picture. Incompetent cleaning, retouches or repairs made during an earlier period may add to his work. In some instances the time required to perform major restorations on a work of little value may prohibit complete restoration.

A code of ethics should be understood between the client and the restorer from the beginning. A client should not attempt to compromise

'The Brontë Sisters' by Patrick Branwell Brontë, painted about 1835. National Portrait Gallery, London. (From left to right) Anne, Emily Jane and Charlotte Brontë. The ghosting portrait of the artist is faintly visible in the centre. One version of the story is that his father scrubbed Branwell's portrait out with alcohol after disowning him. The cracked and flaked lines are the result of the painting having been folded and left on top of a cupboard

the restorer's integrity. The restorer should not be asked to make a painting more accomplished than it was originally, or to improve upon a painting by unwarranted retouching or falsification of the picture in any way.

A painting of value always requires the attention of a professional restorer when cleaning is contemplated. A collector should not attempt to remove varnish from a fine painting. The only way to acquire experience in removing varnish is to practise on old pictures of little value. These can be acquired from sources such as junk shops, picture framers and auctions. Generally they are amateur works or poor copies from the past.

The restorer is often faced with the task of removing previous restorations or making them less obvious. He should not have to contend with rectifying the inept picture repairs and cleaning attempts of the novice.

Restorers are generally reluctant to evaluate the condition of paintings from photographs, or to appraise the value of pictures or provide authentication. However, they may assist the client in an insurance investigation by examining the extent of damage, the proportion of depreciation which the painting may have incurred, and the estimated cost of repair.

Old Paintings

A potential art buyer should always bear in mind that, as in a used car, many faults may underlie the gleaming surface. He must also be aware that paintings which are in a seemingly hopeless condition may be transformed with the attention of a competent restorer. If the buyer acquires some concept of restoring methods, he can buy old paintings cheaply with the knowledge that their poor appearance may be remedied by restoration.

Paintings bought for small sums are frequently cleaned by student restorers for profitable resale. Many dealers in old paintings now recognize this sales potential and prices are increasing. The value of any picture is immediately increased by proper cleaning, repair, and suitable framing.

There are a number of possible defects of which the buyer should be aware when purchasing an old painting. Recognition of these is important in determining the approximate value and life expectancy of a particular work. Chapter VI describes common faults and their probable causes.

Modern Works

Modern paintings not more than thirty years old and freshly painted pictures need a somewhat different approach in their examination. It may be important to judge the materials and technique of the artist to determine whether or not the picture will remain stable. This is a task which even experienced restorers may find difficult.

I have seen Braques and Picassos painted in the late 1930s with dry, loose paint barely attached to the support. During this period artists were experimenting with sand and gravel mixed into the paint for texture. If paintings such as these are not restored, their chances of survival are limited. A few years ago a painting in a museum was noticed to take on a curiously sagging look. The subject was a realistic self-portrait of the artist in the trompe-l'oeil manner. Slowly but surely the entire surface had begun to slide. The picture was then hung upside down in an attempt to reverse the flow, but the damage was done from the moment the artist applied excessive amounts of linseed oil in his painting medium.

One talented contemporary artist built his pictures in a tactile third-dimensional style with successive layers of paint until some of his paintings were as much as four to six inches thick. At the exhibition of his work I noted that these were shown in cases, lying flat. It would not take an expert to foresee the results that standing them upright would have had!

Not only students but artists of international fame sometimes use inferior materials and questionable methods in their paintings. It is perhaps understandable that an artist may achieve a desired effect by using a poor support or medium, and that in these instances his aesthetic considerations take precedence.

Some art galleries guarantee that the price received for a work by one of their stable of artists will not decline in value within a given period. It might be as well if they could offer a guarantee that the work would not unduly deteriorate. When accident or neglect by a third party is the cause of deterioration, no discredit should reflect on the artist.

WORKS ON PAPER

Watercolours, prints and drawings should be inspected for *foxing* (rusty brown spots caused by micro-organisms forming on iron impurities in the paper) and mildew. Discolouration may be due to dirt, dampness or the breakdown of the cellulose fibres. A skilled paper expert is capable of restoring a soiled and torn work almost to its original state. The repairs will be virtually undetectable to the untrained eye.

Many dealers and collectors discard works on paper which they consider to be in a hopeless condition. It is unfortunate that they are usually unaware of the remarkable restorations that can be effected by an expert.

When the collector has located an expert paper restorer, he might speculate by buying art on paper which is sold cheaply because of poor appearance. Some papers are impossible to salvage completely, but even these benefit noticeably by treatment.

Framing

A good picture frame should complement and protect a picture. In addition, it will give the painting greater depth and dimension. Large paintings can appear relatively small, and small pictures large, through a judicious choice of moulding and colour.

In the past, oil picture frames were often enormous, with heavy gilt carving built up of solid wood or plaster. Watercolours were framed in ornate mounts with wide overly decorated mouldings which frequently included scroll work and brass name plates.

Correct fitting of the picture in the frame is important. A picture wedged in too tightly will distort the canvas. The picture should fit with a fractional margin to allow *keying out*. The keys are small triangular wooden wedges that fit into slots at the four joining corners of the stretcher. They are tapped in further to tauten a slackening canvas, or to flatten ripples caused by improper stretching. Care must be taken to avoid tautening the canvas when the slackening may be caused temporarily by dampness. Like most fabrics, canvas responds to atmospheric conditions, becoming tighter in dry weather and looser in dampness.

Sometimes pictures have been put into frames improperly with rust-prone iron nails driven through the canvas edge into the stretcher and frame. Nails hammered part way into the frame and bent over the stretchers may secure the picture in place, but they also increase the risk of damage to the front when being hammered. Nails bent in this way will scratch any picture surface with which they may come in contact.

To facilitate the exchange of paintings and frames after exhibitions, clip fastenings may be screwed into the frame and turned around to hold the picture firmly. Metal plates can be screwed at an angle to each corner of the picture at the back of the frame to assure a more permanent fixture. The use of tin-tacks in stretching a canvas is recommended as a prevention against rust.

When work is being done on a frame reverse, whether to fit screw eyes or to remove the painting, the front should be protected. A folded blanket will safeguard the moulding from scratches and provide a cushion for hammering.

Modern paintings are often framed in a simple and inexpensive manner. Wooden stripping or bagettes may be used to enclose the picture and provide some protection against damage. Metal strips of aluminium or brass make a handsome presentation. Correct mitring of the corners is essential and welded or bevelled corners give a professional look. Metal frames are not easily damaged and scratches are barely discernible, which makes them ideal for travelling exhibitions. Perhaps the most extreme framing of all is, in fact, no frame—merely fabric-masking tape. Perspex (plexiglass) has been moulded to make frames, as well as a picture glass substitute. Although a non-breakable material, it is subject to scratches and abrasions which obscure the underlying work.

Many pictures bought in auctions will have damaged frames. Scratches and chipped areas can be built up with a ready-made gesso and then suitably coloured. Frames having a gold finish or even genuine gold leaf can be touched up with Treasure Gold, an excellent material for simulating gilding. It can be obtained in numerous shades from light to dark. A silver colour is also made for silver frames and mirrors.

Professional framers usually display examples of corner mouldings. A good framer will, in addition, make up his own mouldings to suit the individual picture. He will suggest style, colour, linen or other possibilities. Some craftsmen still make handcarved frames and others specialize in gilding.

The majority of clients are content to be advised by the framer, expecting him to be an expert. Many framers are indeed expert and will provide a frame to enhance the painting. Others are less skilled and the finished frame may be quite incompatible with the painting. Framers, like restorers, do not need qualifications to set up in business.

Mishaps in framing unfortunately occur all too often. I once visited a friend who has some of my prints in his collection. He was particularly keen to hear my opinion of two etchings in expensive new frames. I was appalled to see that the mounts were cut to the edge of the plate marks. No thought had been given to the prescribed one half to three-quarters inch border for original signed prints. At this point the inept framer had realized his mistake and, taking a yellow grease pencil in hand, had boldly forged title, edition number and signature directly on the dark aquatint surface of the prints. I suppose it was in his mind a reasonable course, since he had already trimmed the prints to the edge, thereby reducing their potential value. Original prints are similar to postage stamps in this respect; condition is everything.

Some framers spray varnish on drawings, etchings and watercolours for those clients who are bothered by glass reflections. Indeed, artists' colourmen sell varnish in air-pressurized canisters for this purpose. The works look quite reasonable for a time until they begin to yellow and turn brown. Discoloured varnish is more serious on paper than on primed canvas, as it penetrates the fibres. As this happens over a period of time, the owner usually fails to notice the deterioration.

Paintings and works on paper have been cut down to fit into available frames. It is surprising how seldom the owners notice these atrocities. Perhaps it is because the paintings are newly acquired and immediately sent for framing that the owner's original impression is not retained.

Frame shops lacking adequate storage space can expose pictures to many hazards. Much scuffing results from pictures being shoved into already jammed racks. When leaving a painting to be framed it is advisable to request that easily scratched surfaces should be covered with wrapping paper until actually fitted into the frames. I have had paintings returned from framing covered with paint flecks or sprayed paint. They had obviously been left exposed in a room in which frame finishing had taken place.

Most of us become familiar with paintings through reproductions, and over a period of time consider that certain works are among our favourites. A reproduction can sometimes be considerably misleading. Apart from colour variations, which are almost inevitable, the actual surface quality of a painting can be far less appealing than the reproduction makes it appear. A further illusion may be the size relationship. We may form impressions from art books, perhaps due to composition or scale, that paintings are small when they are in fact large.

It is most disconcerting if, when we first have an opportunity to view a favourite work, the frame is quite unrelated to the painting. Some of the world's leading art museums are guilty of displaying paintings in poor or damaged frames. This may be due to museum administrations accepting a collection intact. They may prefer not to offend the donor by making changes, however desirable. What a vast improvement could be brought about by a small expenditure. It is quite surprising how well some Old Masters look in suitable contemporary frames.

A story is told relating to frames and large collections. It seems that near closing time at the Louvre a prankster flung an empty frame on an inner staircase. Some five days later a relieved staff emerged from a frantic inventory of the collection to find that no painting had been stolen!

PROTECTING THE PICTURE REVERSE

One of the most valuable protections a painting can have is so simple that it is a wonder so few are provided with it. This is a firm hardboard backing,

White spirit wiped gently over the picture for clearer observation. The diagonal line is caused by a stretcher reinforcement pressing against thin unlined canvas

cut to fit at the back of the stretcher. Dust is kept out, direct writing and affixing of gummed labels are rendered harmless, and damage by knocks from the back is prevented.

Although these precautions are taken, there is still an element of risk involved. I recently examined a painting by a modern artist which the owner suspected had been overpainted. The back of the painting was protected by cardboard showing some intention of care. Upon removal of the cardboard, areas of mildew were seen to be growing at the back of the canvas. It was quite evident the painting had been stored in extremely damp surroundings. The backing had, to a degree, accelerated the growth of mildew spores by trapping the moisture. The spores penetrated through to the front of the picture. An attempt had been made to overpaint the area in an effort to eradicate the spots. Unfortunately the retouching extended until most of the original painting had been covered.

In order to avoid the trapping of moisture, two holes at the top and bottom can be cut in the hardboard back, thus allowing the free passage of air so that the canvas may 'breathe'. To prevent dust from entering, the holes can be covered with gauze strips.

A more elaborate means of protecting the picture from atmospheric contamination is to seal it hermetically within a specially constructed box. A fine example of this is a scene of Venice painted by Turner that is in the collection of the Victoria & Albert Museum, London. In the 1880s it was placed in a vacuum-sealed copper box with a glass front. It remains one of the best-preserved of Turner's paintings.

Today a sealed box might be constructed of modern materials, such as perspex incorporating a frame. An important consideration would be the complete drying of the painting and support before sealing. Silicone gel packs can be placed in the box behind the corners of the painting to absorb any residual moisture.

Selecting a Hanging Space for Pictures

The position a painting should occupy in a room is of the utmost importance both aesthetically and to the future preservation of the work. How many paintings have been hung in that long-favoured spot over the fireplace mantel, with the result that each winter a new layer of sooty grime covers the surface? Such an area of obvious focal attention should not necessarily be avoided for picture hanging but the owner must recognize that the deterioration of the picture will be somewhat hastened. Particular watch should be kept for undue alterations in the structure of the paint and support.

I recall the story of a Scots friend who described how his father always carved the Sunday joint on a mantel beside a large painting of the Western Isles. Needless to say the heather received a rich patina of soot and grease over the years. A good deal of future restoration would be avoidable with some forethought.

Paintings hung in kitchens are subjected to grease and acid deposits forming gummy, dust-catching layers. The opening of beer or carbonated drinks sends forth a fine spray which will appear like a spotted blight on the painting. Moisture formed in steam cooking will contribute towards further deterioration.

Paintings should not be hung over radiators, central heating or air vents, if there is a choice of space. Hot air heating vents should be provided with filters to prevent the circulation of dust. In some instances central heating has been responsible for the warping of stretchers, frames and panels. Veneered panelling and furniture have curled and peeled due to exposure to central heating. The normal infiltration of industrial smog, due in great part to carbon monoxide from motor exhausts, is continually increasing. Pollution of the air has had a disastrous effect on paint surfaces and supports.

Sudden and frequent changes in temperature are to be avoided. In themselves they may have little effect on the painting, but they influence the amount of moisture in the room. A constant temperature is most desirable but difficult to maintain without the installation of a hygrometer. Many of these devices are used in museums or public art collections.

Lighting

The effect of light across the picture surface is important in determining the most suitable viewing position. Works hung parallel to windows will probably reflect light. Glazed and highly varnished pictures most certainly will show some reflection. A reflectless glass is marketed, but it has a tendency to diffuse the picture. Varnished pictures can have their reflective appearance minimized by applying specially prepared waxes, after making certain the surface is entirely free from dust and dirt. An application of a matt varnish obtainable from art suppliers will also reduce glare.

Direct sunlight should be avoided. Prolonged exposure will cause the varnish to yellow prematurely or crack. Some nineteenth-century paintings contain bitumen, which will soften in the sun's rays and cause wrinkling. The fading of impermanent pigments will accelerate with exposure. Museums displaying rare books and documents in glass cases keep them protected by sliding drapes, which are opened only for viewing.

The effect of well-placed artificial lighting can be astonishing. I well remember an example of this at Kenwood House, London. For many years I have considered the Rembrandt self-portrait in the Iveagh Bequest to be the finest of the many studies he made. It is a melancholy portrait, capturing the artist towards the end of his great powers and before the decline brought on by age and tribulations. The painting hangs between two windows in the corner of a large room and the light is often disturbing to the viewer. I was confident that I knew this painting in all its aspects. One day I was admiring it when a museum guard arrived with two important visitors. He stepped behind a curtain and flicked the switch of a spotlight located about four yards from the portrait. The immediate impact was like the contrast of night and day. The dark background came alive with colour and the flesh glowed as Rembrandt must have meant it to be seen. I can more fully appreciate the sudden shock a newly cleaned picture has upon a person who has long loved it—dirt, grime, deteriorated varnish and all. It seems we so often cherish the familiar and in consequence cherish much that was not the artist's original intent.

Hanging a Picture

Aesthetic values apart, paintings are purchased with a view towards enhancing a room's interior. In the majority of cases where décor has been the foremost thought, paintings are hung to complement or match the colour of the walls, rugs and furniture. To most artists this is a deplorable situation. They prefer those rare instances when enthusiastic collectors have changed colour schemes to complement selected hues from paintings. Artists always hope that their works will be recognized for something more than being a mere accessory. When the owners move to new surroundings there can be little future for a painting originally purchased to decorate the previous home.

Hanging a picture can be a misery if unforeseen difficulties are encountered. A nail, confidently struck once or twice through plaster, and then suddenly bending, usually indicates a brick wall or possibly a pipe. Tapping the wall gently beforehand for a hollow sound will help find the best point to drive a nail. If blockage proves to be of brick or stone, a masonry drill is essential. A substance such as Polyfilla packed into the now enlarged hole will dry in a few minutes, allowing the nail to be tapped in. Thin walls or false walls will not hold a picture hook securely. Fly-wing screw bolts are available which, when inserted, provide two metal wings that spring open to ensure stability.

Plaster walls can be kept from chipping by crossing two strips of paper-masking tape, knocking a nail through the tape centre into the plaster layer, then removing the tape. This is definitely a landlord pleaser. Should there be nailing restrictions a picture-rail hook may be used. Table-top easels display paintings with the advantages of mobility and ease in changing pictures. Another possibility for hanging lightweight pictures is the use of special adhesive tabs with picture hooks which support weights of fifteen to twenty-five pounds. These are invaluable for hanging on a solid wall, although heavy frames and glass must be avoided.

Prepare the painting for hanging by measuring equal distances from the top and sides for the placement of screw-in picture eyes. A gimlet is handy for making a small initial hole. Picture wire and eyes may be purchased in small fixture packets. The gauge of the wire will depend upon the weight to be supported. If only thin wire is available, it should be doubled for heavy frames. A picture hanging chain can be obtained when necessary.

The strain on wires and eyes should be tested by lifting the picture by the wire. Heavy frames will often bend the picture eyes. To alleviate this, special eyes are made with rings which take the strain off the screw base. The wire should be adjusted so that the picture's weight will not stretch the wire to expose the hook above the picture.

Picture wire is made with numerous strands. The advantage of strand wire over solid wire is that the strands break one by one to give warning that a replacement will be required. Both types are subject to rust and stress. I have found pictures hanging quite literally by a single remaining strand. Excess wire should not be rolled behind the picture as in time it it will bulge the canvas forward.

Pictures should be hung with a slight forward tilt rather than flush against the wall. This will minimize the amount of dust deposited on the surface and leave space for air to circulate behind the painting. Small cleats at the back bottom corners of the frame will project the picture sufficiently to prevent dust from collecting between the picture and the wall.

Pictures should be inspected every year and taken down from the wall to ensure that the hanging wire is intact. Serious damage can result from a wire breaking and the picture dropping to the floor. If the canvas is loose, the keys should be tightened, making sure that a loosened key does not drop between the stretcher bar and canvas at the back. The pressure made by foreign objects such as plaster, labels and tacks falling into this space can be responsible for dents in the fabric and for cracking and flaking of the paint. To remove any foreign objects from between the stretcher bar and canvas, stand the painting in a slightly tilted position. If the object does not drop out, a pliable knife, such as a flat spatula with rounded ends, can be inserted. Dust collecting in the crevice will retain moisture from the atmosphere and result in deterioration of the ground and paint layers.

When dusting is necessary, it should be done with a feather duster or a very soft brush. Unlike furniture and rugs, paintings should not receive daily dusting. Paintings should not be dusted if there is any sign of flaking paint. Great care should be taken with impasto paint ridges which may fracture with only light pressure.

Temporary Repairs

Repairs to paintings are limited by knowledge and equipment. Patching a hole in a painting should be left to the expert. Tears in canvas can be temporarily secured with wide masking tape or adhesive tape. It is recommended that this be done as soon as possible or tears will begin to curl and the paint layers will be compressed and crack. The damaged painting is laid face down on a smooth paper, and the torn section is flattened into place. The frayed fibres can be joined as evenly as possible before applying pressure to the tape strips.

Dents caused by objects or knocks can be flattened. The painting is laid face down on top of water-resistant paper. A small sponge or cloth is dampened in water and applied to the back of the protruding bulge, gently moistening the immediate area without pressure. A white blotter is laid over the area, on top of which is placed a flat smooth surface such as a small hardboard. Weights are then added. The blotter is removed and replaced with a dry one every half hour until the canvas is completely free of moisture. The last blotter and weights should be allowed to remain for about twenty-four hours to ensure the complete flattening of the bulge.

WATER-SOAKED PAINTINGS
Some situations will require immediate attention. Paintings involved in fire or flood will need first aid. The flood in Florence presented the greatest modern catastrophe to art treasures; however, a burst pipe in the home

or the apartment above can also cause water damage. A painting which has become soaked should be removed carefully to a safe place. If it has been exposed to moving water or immersed for some time, there will probably be flaking paint. A careful search should be made of the surroundings to find any missing fragments of paint. These should be kept in an envelope and given to the restorer, who, with the patience of a jig-saw puzzle expert, will try to discover their correct place. The painting should remain in a damp environment until a restorer can examine it. An experienced restorer with laboratory facilities should attend to the drying and consolidating processes. Meanwhile the painting must be kept flat with the face up to prevent further loss of loose paint, as the canvas will begin to shrink and force the paint to flake.

Should the painting be merely splashed or soaked for a brief period, the collector might attempt to dry it. The painting should be laid face down on sheets of waxed or water-resistant paper. Large white blotters of sufficient size to cover the wetted area will be needed. A plate glass, hardboard or any flat rigid surface available should be placed over the blotter. Weights are then placed on top. The damp blotters should be replaced with dry ones about every half hour until the canvas is thoroughly dry. The stretcher keys may then be tightened to stretch the canvas taut.

FIRE DAMAGE

Fire is the most feared of all causes of damage to paintings, yet blackened and blistered paintings have been effectively restored as long as sufficient paint and fabric remain to be attended. During fires, valuable paintings have been thrown from windows with the assumption that damage is a better risk than complete destruction. Handling of a fire-blistered painting requires great delicacy, as the blisters will disintegrate when touched. Apart from protecting the painting, there is little the layman can do until a restorer is contacted.

Chemical fire-extinguishers of the water, soda-acid type will damage paintings. A dry-chemical type with a pressure gauge is preferable. Its lighter weight is advantageous in combating fires near paintings. A carbon-dioxide extinguisher can be used but may leave a chemical deposit on paintings as it must be employed at close range. As toxic fumes are emitted, care must be taken with this type of extinguisher in unventilated rooms. Only small fires can be contained with these portable units. Repairs to damaged paint and supports are dealt with in greater detail in Chapter VII on Consolidation and Repairs.

Insurance

Insuring works of art varies depending upon the country, the individual company, and the type of coverage required. Owners of one or more expensive paintings are often misled into thinking these works will be covered at value under a contents policy. In Britain, under a home protection policy, it states:

> *In the event of the happening of any loss or damage occasioned by any of the Perils specified in Paragraph A(1), (2), (3), (4), (5) and (8) no Stamp Collection, Curio, Picture or other Work of Art shall be deemed of greater value than five per cent of the full value of the Contents as above declared and in the event of the happening of any loss or damage occasioned by any of the Perils specified in Paragraph A(6) and (7) no Stamp Collection, Curio, Picture or other Work of Art or Article of Gold, Silver or other Precious Metal, Jewellery or Fur shall be deemed of greater value than five per cent of the full value of the Contents as above declared unless in each of the said cases the Stamp Collection, article or other object is specially insured in a separate item by this Policy.*

If articles of great value are to be insured a representative will wish to inspect the premises and advise on additional security measures to fulfil the necessary requirements. Window locks and mortice door locks must be fitted. If a collection is of considerable value an electric alarm system may be needed for maximum security. This would certainly be advisable for restorers undertaking private work in their homes.

Insurance companies may be reluctant to pay full coverage in certain situations where there is evidence of insufficient precautions taken to prevent theft or damage.

Paintings in transit can be insured for the period of transport to the exhibition site and back. Some galleries and institutions will insure the work while it is on their premises but not during the course of delivery. Policies with inexpensive premiums can be arranged for these brief periods.

A few years ago I purchased a large work from the Royal Academy which attracted much attention during the summer exhibition. It is constructed of several hundred lengths of coloured strings stretched taut and radiating to precisely placed nails. Elegant old ladies and groups of art students succumbed to the temptation to strum the strings. I immediately took out an insurance policy costing one pound sterling to cover the summer period and the ultimate safe delivery of the work to my studio.

Transport and Packing

Serious damage may occur to paintings during transport. To ensure maximum safety a reliable art transport service is recommended. This will involve some expense but less than the cost of repairs to the painting. It is best to leave paintings framed for added protection.

When transporting a painting personally, one may find a frame inconvenient, particularly if travelling by air or rail. Cumbersome or ornate and easily chipped frames can be removed. A simple strip frame is all that is necessary to provide a carrying edge and protection for the corners and surface of the painting. Four slats, about half an inch thick and two inches wide, should be cut to form a frame round the painting. They are held by two nails in each section allowing an overlap of about half an inch at both the reverse and front sides of the painting. It can then be grasped and carried easily. An enclosed package can be made by taping or tying the frame between two solid sheets of cardboard.

When paintings are being packed for transport, all screw eyes, nails and other projections should be removed to prevent their scratching other picture surfaces. Frame corners can be protected by folded newspapers or corrugated cardboard. If the pictures are under glass, it is advisable to place a few strips of masking tape vertically and horizontally on the glass to help prevent shattering if pressure or movement causes stress.

Some artists carry a small kit for retouching both paintings and frames which may have incurred minor scratches or fingerprints during transit to an art gallery.

Protection for pictures transported by motor vehicle can be made by placing sheets of corrugated cardboard between each picture. Blankets may be used as buffers at the front and sides of the load. Vertical packing is advisable whenever possible. The pictures should be inclined back against the seat so that they will not shift forward while the car is in motion. The rear vision should be kept free from obstruction. I have transported sizeable exhibitions in a carefully packed Volkswagen utilising every space including a roof rack.

During hot weather paintings on wooden panels should not be left in a closed car. I have seen a hardboard panel bowed by the heat, with the result that large flakes of paint have literally popped off. The sun baking on metal roofs can create oven-like conditions. Air temperatures of 75°F can rise inside the car to well over 100°F within half an hour.

PREPARATIONS FOR POSTING

Exhibitions of contemporary paintings may be transported at minimal cost by using sturdy mailing tubes. The paintings are removed from the stretchers and carefully rolled to slide into the tube. A tube of wide diameter can accommodate several paintings at one time. The cost is less than that of sending a single painting flat and crated. If time is a factor air-mail or air freight should be used for expediency and to lessen the chances of damage.

The mailing-tube method of packing should be confined to the works of living artists who know the pliability of their paints. It would be unwise to subject old paintings to this treatment. Old paintings which have been tightly rolled and stored for a long period should be allowed to relax for a short interval in a damp atmosphere such as a cellar. They should not be unrolled by force or the ground will crack and the paint flake.

To roll a contemporary painting, lay it face down on a sheet of waxed or water-resistant paper and roll the two together to prevent the paint surface from coming into contact with the fibres on the reverse. When this method is used the canvas is rolled with the priming and paint side facing outward. Should cracks occur, they will come together again when the canvas is restretched. If the painting is rolled with the paint side inward, tension is created by the paint film being squeezed, resulting in a chipped or wrinkled surface. A painting with heavy impasto or palette-knife texture should not be rolled as some serious cracking is likely.

It is wise to insure works of art which are to be posted against possible damage or loss. The post office or railway express may only insure the parcel for a limited sum. If the value of the painting is greater than this figure, a special fine art risks policy may be taken out privately.

Shipments by post will not be covered by insurance unless the work is in a proper packing. Damage claims resulting from improper packing, such as using a mailing tube of insufficient strength, will be challenged.

CRATING

Paintings on panel, paintings in fragile condition and those requiring shipment complete with frames should be crated. When a painting is prepared for crating, it should be wrapped in waterproof paper with the frame corners padded and enclosed in a cardboard carton for added protection. This will prevent packing materials such as wood shavings or polystyrene synthetic foam from penetrating to the painting. A painting encased in this manner is kept suspended during shipment and will be impervious to shocks caused by rough handling. 'Fragile' labels are no guarantee against rough treatment, but they should always be affixed to the crate.

The crate should be constructed according to the size and weight of the painting. Small works will be reasonably safe in hardboard or plywood crates. Boxboard or similar strong materials are suitable for larger works. If several paintings are to be shipped, care should be taken that the crates are not too heavy. Damage may result from a mishandled heavy crate being dropped. Grooved hand-holds or strongly secured straps would help the movers handle the bulk more safely.

Nails can be used in the construction of the crate up to the point of fitting the lid, which should be attached with screws to facilitate subsequent removal and repacking. In most instances the lid should be at the end rather than at the side of the crate.

CHAPTER II

THE RESTORER

History

'A good picture, like a good fiddle, should be brown.'

This oft quoted statement by Sir George Beaumont, the great nineteenth-century collector and art benefactor, typifies the attitude of his generation towards art. Lack of attention was by no means the worst fate to befall works of art. In the early part of the century, a painting purported to be by Titian was discovered. A panel of experts was called in to investigate and offer their opinions as to its authenticity. When agreement was reached that the style and materials seemed right, a member proposed that pure alcohol be poured directly on to the painting. The reason offered was that if the picture was authentic the age-hardened paint film would not be damaged!

Fortunately scientific advancement in the conservation of works of art has progressed enormously since then. Today the mistakes of the past are rectified by restorers with skills comparable to those of highly trained surgeons. The complexity of modern equipment and techniques would amaze restorers of past generations.

Throughout the ages a few skilled men with foresight have tried to preserve works of art for succeeding generations. Most of their knowledge was based upon the analysis of the technical achievements of early artists as described by such scholars as Pliny and Theophilus. The manuscripts they wrote have been studied closely by restorers to enable them to understand more fully the ancient methods and materials used in the construction of paintings. It was generally assumed until comparatively recent times that the artist was the only person qualified to restore pictures.

One of the earliest establishments which may be compared with modern

The Greek restorer Stavros Mihalarias cleaning a fifteenth-century icon

restoration institutes and laboratories, at least administratively, was established in Venice in the early eighteenth century under the direction of the esteemed painter Domenico Maggiotto. Maggiotto's primary concern was the implementation of the rules and principles laid down by a governing body to control and limit the extent of cleaning and repairs carried out by restorers under his supervision. Prior to this the work of repairs, maintenance and supervision had been carried out to a limited degree by reasonably competent artists or workmen.

Mrs Merrifield recounts in her *Original Treatises on the Arts of Painting* that the noted Venetian restorer Pietro Edwards, directing the restoration of state paintings in Venice during the eighteenth century, observed that many pictures in the collection were considerably darkened by oil and other substances. These films were attributed to copyists who had apparently rubbed the pictures with various mixtures in order to see the true colours more clearly.

Early Restoration Attempts

Some of the early methods used in restoration seem almost incredible to the scientifically trained restorer of today. For example, washing paintings with water was common practice until this century. It was carried out not only by individual restorers but also by many museums on a regular basis, soap generally being used and followed by rubbing with a cloth or cotton wool to dry the painting. Not only does water penetrate very quickly through minute cracks to permeate the ground and size, but the rubbing endangers raised or loose paint.

During this period a number of equally misguided persons formed the opinion that the paint surface might be affected by water and therefore washing should take place on the back of the picture. This eventually led to shrinking or cockling of the canvas and cupping of the paint.

A few early cleaning solvents such as spirits of wine, essential oils and turpentine, when in competent hands, removed varnish effectively. Caustic potash, a strong alkaline, was used by restorers although it was employed cautiously as it often attacked through the varnish to the paint layer. This has been replaced by ammonia. One seventeenth-century restorer actually scoured the varnish from pictures with warm water and smalt, a pigment containing pulverised glass.

Brittle paintings have been subjected to rubbing and shining with rags and linseed oil or by dry rubbing to reconstitute the varnish. They were often soaked from both the front and the back with linseed oil. Pictures have been treated with all sorts of concoctions to bring out or revive their colours. Some of these include butter, machine oil, beer, lard and petroleum jelly.

Newly cleaned pictures were often given an overall toning varnish to obscure colours slightly if they might appear to critics to have been over-cleaned. Another recourse was to frame the picture behind imperfect glass in order to disguise and tone down defective cleaning and retouching. The risk of overcleaning prompted many restorers in the seventeenth and eighteenth centuries to retouch pictures often directly on top of the darkened varnish.

In his book *The Materials of the Artist* Max Doerner relates what is perhaps one of the most ill-fated attempts to remove an old canvas from a painting. The episode Doerner describes is taken from a book written by a restorer in 1834. Doerner writes, 'It is recommended that paper be first pasted over the face of the picture. Then the picture is laid on its face, and a uniform ridge of wax of a finger's breadth is kneaded all around the edge of the back of the canvas. This low-walled tank is then filled with either hydrochloric or nitric acid, which is allowed to remain standing on the canvas until every thread is completely eaten away. If the action of the acid is too slow, it must be strengthened. Later the acid is poured off and the picture rinsed several times with water. This gentleman informs us that his main reason for writing this book was "to stop the practice of restoration by incompetent persons". One becomes curious to know what the incompetent ones did.'

Fortunately not all attempts at art restoration were as inept as some of those mentioned here or we should have considerably fewer works in our collections today.

Restoration as a profession developed very slowly. It was not until scientific aids such as the microscope and later the camera and X-rays came into use that restoring was recognized as a highly skilled technical field that required extensive study and experience to attain expertise. It was no longer sufficient for the restorer to be able merely to paint. With the acquisition of specialized equipment the restorer gained confidence and was able to undertake many operations which had formerly appeared insurmountable.

The scientific equipment and methods available to the restorer are described in detail in Chapter VI on Painting Examination, Part II.

Noted scientists in other fields of research have used their talents to further the cause of art in general and restoration in particular. Among those of the nineteenth century were Pasteur, Faraday and Pettenkofer. Benjamin West, the American-born painter who succeeded Joshua Reynolds as President of the Royal Academy, London, was eminent in restoring circles.

Sir Charles Eastlake, appointed Director of the National Gallery, London, in 1855, was instrumental in the acquisition of important works for the collection. In 1846 Eastlake, then Keeper of the Gallery, was involved in a dispute with critics over the cleaning of pictures by the restorer John Sequier, whose brother William was the first Keeper of the Gallery. John Sequier formulated the cleaning techniques for pictures in the collection. He later caused a furore when, in a six-week period, he cleaned nine paintings. In his defence it may be noted that he practised semi-cleaning, removing the dirt and outer varnish layers only. The layer of varnish left on the painting served to protect it and to give the picture a warm yellow patina so much admired by art connoisseurs of the day. Some of the pictures were cleaned by friction rubbing with the fingers; this technique powders off the deteriorated varnish.

The National Gallery had at that time the unenviable reputation of being the filthiest gallery in Europe. Industrial smoke, haze and fog containing noxious substances made viewing almost impossible. Gas lamps can have added little enhancement. The effect on the pictures was nearly disastrous. At one period, glass was recommended to protect each picture. The National Gallery has come a long way since those days and is now one of the most advanced galleries in Europe.

The Victoria & Albert Museum, London, was one of the earliest crafts museums to employ restorers. The collection includes pictures, metal works, furniture, musical instruments, textiles, ceramics and other varieties of art objects. As the collection grew, craftsmen from the various trades were called in to repair and restore the objects. This eventually led to a select group being employed in a full-time capacity. Today, as restorers within the Civil Service structure, they work in individual departments well equipped for their particular specialities.

The international aspect of compiling restoration information has been greatly increased by the cooperation of individuals and countries faced by similar problems. Conferences held are attended by the leading restorers of all nations concerned with the preservation of their cultural properties, and are followed by the exchange of ideas through correspondence often resulting in visits between laboratories being arranged for student restorers.

Many of the world's leading museums and galleries have established their own departments of conservation with scientific sections devoted to research. The Louvre laboratory has, for example, provided the art world with a wealth of information about masterpieces in their collection and discoveries of a wider scope made during testing and research programmes.

Training

The restoring profession is not so well known that children voice a desire to be restorers when they grow up. Yet the time may not be far off when this is quite feasible. In the past restorers have generally been recruited from the ranks of artists who have been introduced to the subject in a few specialized art schools or through apprenticeships to private restorers.

A restorer must act from a position of personal integrity. Few people will be able to tell if he has restored a picture to excess. He must be imbued with the inner conviction of his vocation to preserve works of art with the maximum skill that he possesses. He must be equally at home with the paint brush and the microscope. A knowledge of chemistry and physics must be combined with an extensive knowledge of artists' techniques and materials, art history and a sensitivity to painting styles.

Institutions with public collections have generally led the field in techno-logical advancement. Restorers work within the boundaries of established procedures, perfecting techniques and exploring methods for use in the future. Training in museums is practical, but advancement in skill is often dependent upon the type of work the new recruit is allowed to perform. Well-known private or trade restorers provide a training ground for apprentices who, with diligence, may surpass their masters in skill. Only a few schools exist with a curriculum directly providing a training course for restorers. Some of the work in these schools must remain hypothetical as pictures of quality are seldom available for restoring.

A common controversy has been whether an aspiring restorer should have an aptitude for art or science. A criticism sometimes levelled at the artist/restorer is that his lack of scientific knowledge may retard the development of restoring techniques, while on the other hand the scientist/restorer may become so engrossed in theory and experimentation that he may neglect the practical work of restoring. There can be little doubt that equal training in both spheres is essential. The restorer must possess, in addition to skill, a high degree of patience to work for long periods at tedious and precise tasks. Frequently more time is spent on restoring a painting than the artist originally took to paint it!

Scientific apparatus designed for industrial, medical or other specialized jobs has been found adaptable to painting restoration. Were it not for the scientific training and interest of some restorers, valuable aids might not have been discovered and developed.

Restorer and *conservator* are labels which generally embody the same activity. Conservation, a relatively new description of the restorer's expanded duties, has not yet had the stigma attached to it that for many years has been unjustly associated with restoration. Conservator more aptly describes the increased responsibilities of the modern restorer, but for ease and familiarity I use *restorer* in this text.

A room of the Conservation Laboratory at the Los Angeles County Museum of Art. A Zeiss stereoscope is in the right foreground. In the background is a spray booth for varnishing paintings

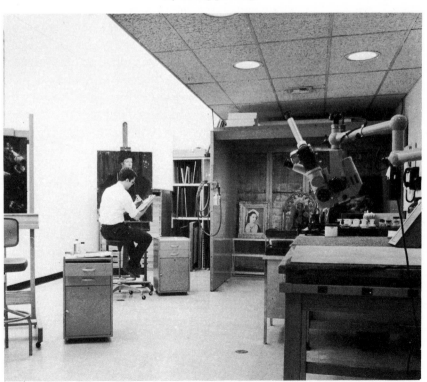

Institutional Duties

A restorer responsible for a collection in an institution has a variety of duties. The paintings must be regularly inspected for any signs of deterioration. He is required to conserve and maintain all works in his care. He will repair and restore paintings in a deteriorating condition with the utmost regard for the preservation of the work and the artist's original conception. He must inspect new acquisitions and, in museums with a small staff, he may be required to aid in the preparation of catalogues and the assembling of exhibitions. Travelling to inspect collections may be involved if the museum offers a restoration service for smaller institutions in the area. He must prepare reports on the condition and treatment of every picture requiring restoration.

New acquisitions must be dealt with as they arrive. Museums normally continue to acquire additions to their collection through purchase and gifts. Whole private collections may be given or left to the museum by benefactors who may have chosen that particular institution in the knowledge that their gifts will be properly maintained.

Restorers are sometimes appointed curators of museums. The curator is responsible for the presentation, care and safety of objects in the museum and for the training of staff. The curator of a museum might be compared with the captain of a ship; any mistake made by a staff member may ultimately be the responsibility of the curator. He must assure the correct physical environment of the gallery and storage area, control air pollution and humidity changes, and arrange correct lighting effects. He must provide security against deliberate damage, theft, fire or indiscriminate hazards. The curator will meet frequently with the restorers on his staff and, if it is a large institution, he may appoint a senior research officer to investigate new methods and materials which might be of use in the various departments. He may arrange for visitors to be conducted through the laboratories and offer limited periods of instruction for members of other institutions.

Institutional Restorers and Trade Restorers

The term *trade* or *commercial* restorer usually describes one who is either employed by a firm or self-employed.

The commercial restorer, depending on his skill and contacts, can receive considerably more remuneration than his institutional colleague.

Time is an important factor to the trade restorer when overhead costs have to be maintained and deadlines must be met for the completion of work.

The Civil Service restorer working in a museum laboratory at a yearly salary with increment and pension prospects has a security advantage over his fellows in the world of commerce. The museum restorer has a certain freedom of activity. He is generally allowed ample time to complete work and is encouraged to investigate new materials and to conduct experiments. He may further himself and the institution through lectures and articles concerned with presenting theory or practical information to select groups.

In either sphere, the integrity and skill of the individual is paramount. An ethical restorer will carry out his work with the highest standard of conservation skill regardless of his circumstances of employment.

Both museum and trade restorers often allocate work to specialists. This is especially true when space and facilities are lacking. Consolidation jobs such as lining and transfer are frequently undertaken by experts who specialize in this work. Technicians may be employed to take and process radiographs (X-rays) and photographs. Framing and mount cutting are largely tendered to firms.

Artists and Restorers

Often contemporary artists are interested in· obtaining desired painting effects without giving proper consideration to the permanency of their materials. Artists have always profited from noting the technical errors of previous generations and discarded harmful methods and materials. Painting was an accomplishment. Long apprenticeships in the service of a master, often doing menial tasks, were required before an artist learned his trade. Paintings were the result of fine craftsmanship. They were constructed layer upon layer, with each layer of priming, paint or glaze bonded one to the other.

After centuries of respect for finely constructed paintings, traditional care and thought in creating pictures for future generations seem to be out of fashion. Contemporary art opinion is more interested in art for the moment, not art for posterity. In the 1950s some art students felt that art for them really began with abstract expressionist painting. Therefore, in their view, the study of early techniques was irrelevant. The results of this attitude will continue to plague restorers for some time to come.

The abandonment of traditional procedures has been of benefit to the semi-tutored and unskilled. Today it is within the capabilities of anyone to be an artist. We live in an age when an ape is considered by some to paint as well as a man, and the work of a five-year-old is compared with the modern masters. The appreciation of craftsmanship and involvement in technical perfection will, it is hoped, eventually overcome the fads and fancies currently fashionable.

Every day science is producing new materials to amaze and confound the artist. Like the restorer, he must become aware of their potentialities and permanence if he is to make constructive use of them.

The new synthetic materials available to painters, printmakers and sculptors have revived the tradition of employing helpers. The Old Masters were in complete technical and aesthetic command of their assistants' work, which is not always feasible with contemporary materials. Modern sculptors, for example, must work in close harmony with the craftsman who is an expert in the particular material the sculptor has chosen. Unless the sculptor apprentices himself to the craftsman, he will have little idea of the actual construction of his envisaged creation.

'Auto-destructive' art is a most appropriate label for a popular trend in the art anti-art circle, yet much of the work being created today is self-destructive quite without intention. Unsound methods and materials are sometimes used in important works which may render them beyond restoration.

Perhaps the most valuable aid the artist could supply the restorer is a documented list of the materials he has used to create his painting. He should describe the support, ground, medium and varnish. Additional information could be adhered to the reverse of the support which might advise a future owner on care and preservation of the painting. This could include dusting procedure, warning of possible heat or moisture damage and other pertinent facts.

The artist should become aware of the explorations in the field of restoration technology. Science and industry are supplying a continual range of new products for the artist. With the introduction of these materials, new concepts and techniques of application are required. Unfortunately the contemporary artist and the restorer are seldom aware of each other's problems. The close relationship of the artist and the restorer is more important than ever before. Artists are seldom knowledgeable about the processes of deterioration, care and preservation. Inevitably the work of an artist becomes subject to restoration. Frequently, and often embarrassingly, these restorations take place within the artist's own lifetime.

Selecting a Restorer

The choice of a restorer depends upon the particular work requiring treatment. There are specialists in stone, metal, wood, tapestry and all varieties of art objects. Within these categories there are restorers who have particular interests. There are, for instance, restorers in ceramics with a Ming Dynasty expertise, painting restorers with a nineteenth-century speciality or those who undertake work by Old Masters. The restoration of photographs is a relatively new field requiring special knowledge and techniques.

Occasionally people are baffled about where to take pictures for restoration. They may decide to stop at a frame shop offering a restoring service. Although the service may be competent, the prospective client would be well advised to seek an unbiased opinion of their skill. Caution should be taken if the restorer claims to clean and repair all types of objects. The restorer chosen should, after examination of the painting, advise the client as to the condition of the picture, the remedy and an estimate of the charge. A further point which may be of importance to the client is the approximate length of time the restoration will take.

Conservation of art is not a licensed profession. Anyone can undertake restoring and advertise his services. Some do so with an overly optimistic regard for their own abilities. The client should be aware that untold damage can be done to paintings and art objects in incompetent hands.

Restorers might act in a secretive manner about their work, enshrouding it with an aura of mystique. Sometimes they do so because they are afraid their methods will be disapproved of by others in the profession. Occasionally they are secretive because of an ill-conceived fear that competitors will copy their recipes.

Art museums are usually helpful when their recommendations are asked regarding a restorer to undertake private commissions. If they do not recommend members of their own staffs, they may offer the names of responsible restorers and firms or advise of organizations to contact whose members are restorers.

London offers the greatest concentration of restoration experts and research laboratories in the world. The National Gallery, the British Museum, the Tate Gallery and the Victoria & Albert Museum are but a few. Most of these will answer queries about fine art and antiquities within their scope. They are not prepared to authenticate works or offer price estimates.

Two organizations established to represent restorers may be able to offer advice; they are The Association of British Picture Restorers and The International Institution for the Conservation of Historical & Artistic Works. The latter was formed in 1950 to bring restorers together in an effort to maintain professional standards and codes of conduct. The Institution is in London. Among its many publications is the quarterly *Studies in Conservation*, in which learned theories are projected together with practical advice and reviews of books dealing with conservation. Meetings are held regularly with lectures on such varied topics as radiography, forgeries and woodworm.

The Institution has a world-wide membership. Associate membership is open to individuals. Institutional membership for museums, libraries, universities and professional institutions is offered. Membership on an associate basis does not necessarily imply expertise but it does indicate a level of professional interest. Fellows of the Institution are chosen from outstanding members of their profession. Many of them are engaged in museum work, teaching or private commissions involving works of quality.

The Association of British Picture Restorers in London is a group of practising restorers dealing with oil paintings only. The organization was formed in 1943 in order to ensure high standards of restoration. New members are admitted after examination by the council. Enquiries from prospective clients are given to London members in rotation. Work in the provinces is assigned to the member living nearest to the client.

Conservation Institutions

At present the number of skilled restorers available in the international conservation field is unable to cope with the backlog of works from antiquity to modern times in need of restoration. The catastrophe to the Florentine Renaissance treasures during the 1966 flood created a crisis in the conservation world. The lesson was two-fold. First, a universal standard must be implemented to provide reasonable safety for works of art in world institutions and public collections. Secondly, institutions should be organized to teach a nucleus of young aspiring restorers. The implementation of this scheme could be brought about through universities arranging a programme of studies leading to a degree of proficiency both on undergraduate and graduate level.

The institutions already engaged in conservation training should expand their facilities and increase student enrolment wherever possible. At present, the institutions which offer training can accept only a limited number of students. No diploma can guarantee expertise, but it does indicate a level of achievement.

A SUMMARY LIST OF INSTITUTIONS OFFERING CONSERVATION TRAINING

BRUSSELS

Institut Royal du Patrimoine Artistique, 1 Parc Cinquantenaire 4, Brussels, Belgium.

The institute serves as a centre for restoration in Belgium. Training courses are offered in the techniques of restoration. Particular concentration is centred upon Flemish Primitive paintings.

LONDON

Courtauld Institute of Art (University of London), 20 Portman Square, London W1.

Established in 1932 as a university institute primarily for the study of art history, the Courtauld Institute now offers a training programme for restorers in the Department of Technology. This department, under the direction of an eminent scientist/restorer, is renowned for the laboratory examination of paintings and materials with particular emphasis on X-rays.
The National Gallery, Trafalgar Square, London WC1.

A four-year training programme for student restorers has been inaugurated at the National Gallery in association with the Tate Gallery and the Victoria & Albert Museum. During the course of study, two selected students at each institute are appointed temporary members of the staff and paid while learning. Vacancies are advertised and applications are accepted during this period only.

MEXICO CITY

The Paul Coremans Centre, Mexico City, Mexico.

This centre was founded under the joint auspices of UNESCO and the Mexican government. It is well equipped with modern apparatus for the examination and treatment of works of art. Training is given to students from Latin America as technicians and conservators. UNESCO has helped to establish similar regional centres in Jos, Nigeria; Honolulu, Hawaii; and New Delhi, India.

MUNICH

The Doerner Institute, Meiserstrasse 10, Munich 2, Germany.

Founded in 1937, training in picture restoring is given as well as research into painting materials and techniques. The institute is named after Max Doerner, who spent his life researching and writing on these subjects.

NEW YORK

The Conservation Center of the Institute of Fine Arts (New York University), 1 East 78th Street, New York, NY 10021.

Established in 1961, the Conservation Center offers a four-year course covering a broad area of restoration categories. Students use traditional painting materials and methods to explore the techniques of the masters. They examine and treat objects in various categories from easel paintings and drawings to glass, metal, ceramics and frescoes. Courses in the structure, materials and technology of works of art are included. The final two years are spent on concentrated research in a particular specialization. Seven months of this time are given to a full-time internship with an established restorer.

The State University College at Oneonta, c/o The New York State Historical Association, Cooperstown, New York 13326.

The college offers a three-year graduate course in the conservation of historic and artistic works, leading to a Master's Degree. This newly instituted course is located in a building provided by the State University of New York. Two members of the faculty are Mr and Mrs Sheldon Keck, well-known American restorers. Lectures, demonstrations and seminars are combined with laboratory-workshop practice, followed by a one-year internship under the supervision of an established conservator.

ROME

The Rome Centre (International Centre for the Study of the Preservation and the Restoration of Cultural Property), 256 via Cavour, Rome, Italy.

In 1959 the General Conference of UNESCO established the Rome Centre to unite those interested in the preservation of cultural properties. The centre acts as a storehouse for the exchange of scientific information and publishes papers and books on varied conservation subjects. They do not have a training or research programme but they are helpful in providing lists of the international teaching institutes.

The Instituto Centrale del Restauro, Piazza S. Francesco di Paolo, 9 Rome, Italy.

This, the central institute for conservation in Italy has a special interest in the treatment of frescoes. Research and restoration training are provided.

STUTTGART

Staatliche Akademie der Bildenden Kunste, Am Weissenhof 1, Stuttgart, Germany.

Incorporating a laboratory and a training school in restoration techniques, the academy is devoted to research and teaching. The laboratory was originally founded to research paint constituents and instruct the students of the Academy in painting materials and techniques. The emphasis is now on the investigation of conservation processes and artists' materials, both historical and modern.

VIENNA

Akademie der Bildenden Kunste, Schillerplatz 3, Vienna, Austria.

A training programme in painting restoration and technology is provided at the Academy.

CHAPTER III

PAINTING STRUCTURE AND SUPPORTS

The potential permanency of a painting is dependent upon the bond or cohesion of the support, ground, paint and varnish layer, one to another. Any alteration occurring in one layer affects the stability of those above or below it. Defects in the materials used or their incorrect application by the artist serve to hasten the loss of resilience. A painting does not remain static. Constant expansion and contraction of the support which is continually absorbing and releasing moisture subject the layers to strain.

Modern central heating has accelerated the deterioration of paintings. This convenience was designed to enhance man's personal comfort without regard for the hazards to pictures or wooden furniture. Paintings whose laminated structure is ageing are not sufficiently flexible to withstand the artificially heated atmosphere.

The simplest form of painting structure is a watercolour; a sheet of paper provides a support for the paint. The support and paint layers are the only two essential elements of a watercolour painting. Wooden panels and canvas require additional structural layers to insure their stability. By the Middle Ages the criteria for constructing a painting on these supports were firmly established. Panels, for example, were prepared with layers of soft or hard gesso, some with fabrics embedded in the ground, others were made to receive gold leaf for tooling and burnishing. The method of applying the various layers differed widely between artists but generally their order of construction was similar.

The Anatomy of an Oil Painting on Canvas

The canvas support is first sized with a water-soluble adhesive, such as rabbit-skin glue, for quick drying and to prevent the absorption of oil.

Next, a ground is prepared from white pigments, chalk, gypsum or china clay. The grounds of most prepared canvas today are oil based with white pigments such as zinc or titanium white or white lead combined with chalk. Gesso grounds are reserved primarily for wood panels. The ground must adhere firmly to the support and be suitable to receive the paint, neither too absorbent nor resistant. In the physical structure of a picture, the ground acts as a foundation for receiving paint. Colour may be added to the ground in mixing or applied directly on top of the ground in a thin wash.

The canvas, prepared and stretched, is ready to receive the design and paint layers. The design may be drawn with charcoal or graphite, or painted in turpentine-thinned pigment, usually an umber or sienna.

An underpainting may be used to establish the composition and to influence the tonality of overpainted colours. Underpainting with earth pigments such as ochres and umbers imparts a warming tone; blues and greys have a cooling effect. Sometimes the artist will let these colours bleed through to create certain optical nuances.

A painting medium is a drying oil with a capacity to form a hard durable film. These are generally obtained from linseed, flax seed or poppy seed. Artists usually combine a proportion of turpentine and varnish for fluidity. A dry pigment colour becomes a paint when it is combined with a painting medium. This medium serves as a binder and vehicle for the powder pigment particles which may be fine or coarse, depending on the degree of grinding. The medium may disperse the pigments thinly or allow them to cluster on the canvas. A painting medium is sometimes brushed on an overly absorbent ground to control the absorption of the paint. Wax and lacquer have proved the most permanent binding mediums used in the past.

Oil paints may be applied in thick slabs, smooth or textured layers or in thin transparent glazes appearing not unlike watercolour. A medium containing varnish will impart a gloss to the colours. Paints applied with only turpentine as a vehicle will dry with a dull appearance, which is most evident in the earth colours.

To protect the painting, a final surface coating of varnish is applied, which varnish may be of oil or resin but oil is seldom used today. Resin varnishes are made from natural sources or by synthetic processes. Waxes may be introduced into the varnish or applied over it as an additional surface coating.

Supports

The foundation of a painting is the support. Any description of the anatomy of a painting must begin with this key part of the structure. A painting support may be defined as the physical structure carrying the ground and the additional layers of paint and varnish. The majority of supports are of either wood (rigid) or fabric (flexible) of natural cellulose fibre composition.

The successful treatment of a work of art may be determined by the suitability of the support chosen. An unwise choice of material for a support may contribute to the early deterioration of the painting.

AUXILIARY SUPPORTS

The stretcher to which the canvas is affixed is an auxiliary support consisting of four slats joined at the corners like a frame. They are made expandable by the insertion of wooden wedges or keys in the slotted corners. Tapping in the keys at all four corners tightens and smoothes a loose canvas.

An auxiliary support for canvas that is nailed or otherwise permanently fixed at the corners is called a strainer. These cannot be enlarged to take up slackness. Stretchers or strainers of large dimension are generally provided with a cross bar to strengthen them against warping.

Fabric Supports

Fabric, when used as a term to describe a painting support, is generally synonymous with canvas. Fabric may more specifically mean that the threads are interwoven but neither term indicates the material source of the fibres. *Canvas* is accepted as best describing a coarse cloth made from cotton, hemp or flax used as a support for paintings primarily in Europe and North America.

Fabrics have varied origins of animal, vegetable or man-made nature. The animal fibres come from animal hairs or from insects such as the silkworm. Those of vegetable origin include fibres from plant stems and vegetable hairs. The man-made fibres fall into many categories such as nylon, rayon or more recently developed synthetic materials. A true picture of their suitability as painting supports has yet to be ascertained.

The advantages of fabric supports such as cotton or linen canvas are multiple; light in weight, flexible and reasonably durable to exposure, they remain the most popular support for painting. There are a variety of textures and sizes obtainable and the paint control on a resilient fabric surface is often preferred to that of an unyielding wooden panel.

One of the disadvantages of fabric supports is that animal glues used to seal the fabric for painting abet deterioration. The glue size may encourage

The London studio of the Greek restorer Stavros Mihalarias

mould growth, may become brittle, or may be penetrated by moisture which will subsequently swell and weaken the structure. Unlike wooden panels, the fabric may be torn, dented or permeated from the back unless protection is provided.

The weaving of the threads of a fabric can be quite important to the artist. Small knots in cotton or linen canvas appear on the surface as protuberances in the ground and consequently in the paint layer. These can be quite troublesome particularly when they appear as blemishes in an otherwise beautiful rendering of flesh. Portrait painters would be stricken to find a protuberance of this nature appearing on the nose of an elegant lady.

CANVAS

BURLAP   A heavy, coarse cloth with strands woven from the fibres of the jute plant. It is sometimes referred to as hessian. The natural colour is a light tan. It is generally used to make bags for agricultural and industrial produce. Burlap has been used by many artists, seldom for its texture but often as an economic necessity.

COTTON   The fibres of the cotton plant are nearly pure cellulose. They are used to produce hundreds of products. Those of particular use as a support for paintings include paper, cotton canvas and duck (a lightweight, waterproof canvas). Cotton canvas is relatively new. It has proved the most universally popular support in this century. Cotton is not as durable as linen but it is cheaper and takes the application of paint equally well. Paintings on cotton canvas will probably require lining before those on linen.

HEMP   Derived from fibrous stems, hemp has long been used to make ropes and sailcloth. Finer varieties have been spun into textiles. It is not an ideal painting support but both hemp and jute have been used occasionally since the nineteenth century.

LINEN   A cloth made from the fibres of the flax plant, linen was used for the wrapping of Egyptian mummies. Linen canvases have proved themselves to be strong and enduring painting supports. Like cotton, they vary in weight and strength according to manufacture. Linen products range from fine handkerchiefs and doilies to heavy sailcloth, sacking and tarpaulin.

SILK

One of the principal painting supports of the East, silk is somewhat of a rarity in European painting. Silk is used in restoration as a semi-transparent lining to strengthen ageing documents.

Paintings on silk or fabric may be removed from their auxiliary supports for storage or transportation. Within limits, some may be rolled more permanently. Chinese paintings on silk were wound on cylinders to be opened like scrolls. Although they were often many yards in length they could be stored in a small space.

ACADEMY BOARD

Not a board in the sense that wood is employed in its manufacture, academy board is a hard-pressed pasteboard made of cheap yarn, rope or similar fibres. The ground is prepared with an oil, lead and chalk mixture. During manufacture the surface may be given a fine or rough texture by a paper pressed into the damp ground and removed, leaving an impression. Academy board is a popular painting surface for art students.

CANVAS BOARD

Similar in composition to academy board, canvas board is rather more substantial. A primed canvas is attached to cardboard, turned over the edges, and adhered to the back.

OIL-SKETCHING BOARD

A cheap board for oil sketching is made by pasting paper, with the surface grained to imitate the weave of canvas, on to millboard. Paper without the millboard support is sold in individual sheets or rolls as oil-sketching paper.

CARDBOARD

Various pressed or laminated layer boards composed of fibres may be described as cardboard. They include strawboard, chipboard, poster and illustration board; in fact, any card made for whatever purpose. All have been used as painting surfaces. Few are equal to the task in respect of their lasting durability. I have seen, exposed to the atmosphere, expensively priced paintings on cardboard by a modern master that will be fortunate to survive this century.

Paintings on cardboard, like paintings on wood or fabric, are subject to surface deteriorations. Cardboard is prone to the same problems as those inherent in paper. Dampness may cause buckling and disintegration. Acidity in the cardboard leads to weakening of the fibre structure. The

'*A Woman*' (*detail*) *by Robert Campin* (*1378-1444*). *Reproduced by courtesy of the Trustees, the National Gallery, London. An example of craquelure in an early painting on oak panel. Fine structural age cracking does not interfere with the appearance of the picture*

corners are easily damaged unless they are protected by a frame. In spite of these drawbacks, cardboard may last for many years if properly framed under glass and kept in a reasonable atmosphere.

PAPER

Paper is not strictly a fabric support as defined by strands woven in a predetermined arrangement. The fibres of handmade papers are teased from cotton or linen rags and intertwined in irregular masses. Machine-made papers are similarly irregular in their composition.

I have used oil paints on rough 140-pound paper to achieve an effect which is indistinguishable from waterbased gouache. Unsized papers absorb the linseed oil and varnish in prepared pigments. Hot-pressed papers, or those containing an excessive amount of size and therefore less absorbent, will cause a tell-tale oil stain to creep from the paint edges. In the course of time this will become more pronounced.

Clay and chalk grounds are sometimes applied to paper to render it more receptive to drawing or painting media. An example is paper prepared with a clay base for drawings in silver-point (a thin, silver tip or wire mounted on a wooden handle).

Wood Supports

Wood has been used as a painting support for thousands of years. Long before easel paintings became popular, painted art work on wood was used to add decorative embellishments to man's environment. Early Egyptian painted wood sculptures and encaustic sarcophagi portraits from the Fayum district still exist.

In the Middle Ages wood was the principal painted decoration in cathedrals. Panel paintings of religious subjects painted for altarpieces in the form of diptychs (hinged double-panelled pictures) or triptychs (hinged triple-panelled pictures) form the bulk of our art legacy from this period. Miniature versions of altarpiece paintings were popular for display in the home and for religious pilgrims to carry on journeys.

Paintings on wooden panels are extremely durable if kept in a reasonable environment. A consistent atmosphere is essential to their well-being, rapid fluctuations of temperature tending to cause the most severe damage. The principal disadvantages inherent in wood supports are a tendency to split and warp along the grain lines and their vulnerability to insect infestation and moisture. To be properly seasoned, a wood should be allowed to dry slowly for years. The artist should choose a wood for painting which is completely dry. If the wood is still green, it will shrink as it dries, with disastrous effects on the ground and paint films. Cracking, warping or checking may occur to a panel used in an unseasoned state.

A Summary List of Natural Woods Used in Paintings from the 15th Century Onward

CEDAR The cedar of Lebanon is the only true cedar tree. It was used extensively in Egypt and occasionally in later European panels. It may be subject to shrinkage and warping.

CHESTNUT Ubiquitous in Europe, the chestnut is now nearly extinct in the United States due to blight. It is a strong, soft and light wood, not apt to shrink or warp, although it is vulnerable to worm attack. Chestnut was one of the woods most favoured for panels by Italian artists.

FIR The firs are common to Norway and the southern mountain ranges of Europe. Fir is a soft wood, similar to pine, that was used for German and Flemish paintings.

LINDEN The popular linden tree was used for panel paintings by German, Flemish and Italian artists.

MAHOGANY Until it was imported in quantity from the tropical regions of the Americas, mahogany achieved little significance as a painting surface. Rich in colour and relatively resistant to shrinkage and worm infestation, it is an excellent wood for cabinet-making.

OAK Easily distinguishable by clearly marked annual rings, oak is hard and durable. Species are found in both Europe and North America. Oak was the most popular wood with Flemish artists.

PINE There are many varieties of pine. They may be divided into soft or hard groups depending upon their structure. Pine was extensively used in European panel painting. It warps little and is durable. Resinous exudes from an unseasoned pine panel may occasionally penetrate the painting's structure and cause discolouration.

POPLAR A light, soft wood with fine grain, poplar was used extensively by

Italian painters. The poplar grows in most parts of Europe and North America. It was employed to a lesser degree for panel paintings by the French, who favoured the wood of fruit-bearing trees.

WALNUT   A hard wood found in many parts of the world, walnut is employed widely in furniture making. The colour varies from light to chocolate brown. It has little tendency to warp. Walnut was used occasionally for panels by all the European schools of painting.

Composition Boards

Hardboard, an artificially made fibre building board, is the most widely used support for painting of the composition boards manufactured today. Hardboard is made from pine woodchip fibres obtained by a process of steam pressure explosion. Heat and pressure reform the fibres together. One side is rough, resembling the weave of canvas. This pattern is created by the wire mesh on which the board lies while being formed. Either the rough or smooth side may be prepared with a ground for painting, depending upon the artist's preference for texture. Unlike the natural wood panels, hardboard cannot discolour pigments with resinous exudes. Some hardboards are so poorly made that the corners may be bent with the fingers. The best quality of hardboard available in Britain is generally of Swedish manufacture.

Sundeala board is perhaps the best composition painting support available. Like other composition boards it is made in varying quality, the best being more rigid and durable than hardboard. Its great advantage lies in its light weight, which is useful for large paintings, and it is an excellent support for the marouflage or transfer of paintings. Sundeala may be obtained, like hardboard, in eight by four foot sheets in a variety of thicknesses.

Laminated building boards, such as plywood, are sometimes used as painting supports. The laminated board is made from separate sheets glued together. Its durability and strength depend upon the adhesion of these plies. They are rendered water-resistant by sizing with rosin while being formed. Afterwards oils, waxes or paints are applied to increase resistance. Both sides of the exterior may be covered with laminated sheets of superior quality to those of the core.

Miscellaneous Supports

The urge to create inspired the cave paintings of early man. Lacking the knowledge to make a support, he chose the first surface at hand. Actually this is not too different from the practice of many artists of today, who tend to paint on any surface available.

Supports for paints are many and varied. Clay has been fashioned into plates or vases and painted with coloured glazes for firing. Lacquer paints are applied to papier mâché boxes. Plastic and other synthetic materials are being used increasingly. Paintings on black velvet are a popular form in modern Polynesia.

METAL

Copper, beaten or rolled into sheets, was used as a base for painting from the sixteenth century onward. Few painters employ it today other than as a novel experiment. Copper in sheet form is used as a metal for etching in acid or engraving with burins. Other metals such as iron, which is rust prone, zinc, tin and steel have been used infrequently for painting.

Metal supports, having been found by early experiments to effect chemical changes in some colour pigment, ceased to be of interest to painters. Aluminium and new alloys have revived the use of metal as a support.

Special effects obtained with modern synthetic paints and resins are responsible for the contemporary use of these lightweight metals. Aluminium and brass strips are employed extensively in framing modern paintings.

STONE

Stone is one of the oldest forms of painting support, dating from the dawn of man's evolution. It was replaced by tree bark and eventually by woven or pressed natural fibres. Stone, other than that used for walls, has rarely been employed as a painting surface since medieval times. Small pictures may be found painted on marble, slate, agate, and a variety of stone surfaces. Lapis lazuli, malachite and other stones and minerals have been ground to make artists' pigments. Porous stone of calcium carbonate composition found chiefly in Bavaria are used for drawing and printing lithographs.

PLASTER

The most widely known paintings on plaster are frescoes, which are discussed in Chapter V on Painting Media and Technique. Some plaster works have survived as independent easel paintings such as the compositions of Fra Filippo Lippi. Plaster is made of sand and a cementing material such as lime plaster or gypsum plaster mixed with water. Long hair from cattle and natural fibres may be added to strengthen the consistency.

LEATHER

Historical documents refer to the use of leather stretched on a panel for painting. The practice occurs infrequently after the sixteenth century. Leather objects such as shields, saddles and casks were sometimes painted decoratively. Gilding, stamping and tooling of ornate designs were more popular practices. Skins from a variety of animals, prepared by tanning, have been tried as painting surfaces without favourable results. The notable exception is parchment, widely used for illuminated manuscripts, documents and occasionally small-scale paintings.

GLASS

Painting on glass using both oils and watercolours has been practised since the Middle Ages. The motive has usually been to imitate the effect of stained-glass windows. Their application is in the reverse order of normal painting; highlights are painted first on the back of the glass followed by middle values and background. The forms and composition are generally simple in conception. Light from a source behind the glass passes through the thinly painted transparent colours to create a brilliant luminosity. The paint remains stable with the protection of the rigid glass, although moisture may cause flaking. In recent years glass painting has become mainly a decorative art practised by European peasants on an almost mass production scale. The themes are usually of a religious nature.

In the eighteenth century Thomas Gainsborough RA painted several oils on glass to be viewed in a specially constructed show box. The sources of illumination were candles set in holders behind the glass plates. The two foot square oak box had a movable carriage and adjustable lens together with a screen of watered silk for diffusing light. The most effective of these glass paintings are two night scenes bathed in moonlight entitled 'A Pond and Sheep' and 'A Cottage in the Moonlight'. The series of paintings is displayed at the Victoria & Albert Museum, London, in a case with electric illumination providing the visual effect Gainsborough intended.

GLASS PRINTS

A technique for transferring prints to glass and painting them with oils flourished in the eighteenth century. Mezzotints and engravings were held with a coat of varnish face down on to crown glass. The dampened back of the print was rubbed with the fingers until the printed ink and a thin layer of paper were all that remained. Oil paints were applied at the back to the appropriate areas of the print. Sporting prints, marine views and scenes of gay life were popular subjects for this process.

Mechanical colour reproduction methods brought about a decline in the production of glass prints in the nineteenth century. The technique is currently being revived by a few artists' studios in association with interior decorators.

IVORY

Primitive cultures have long used ivory as a carving material. In our modern society ivory has been employed in making a variety of articles from dice to piano keys.

Ivory was once a fashionable and expensive base for the painting of miniatures. A flourishing school was established during the seventeenth and eighteenth centuries to satisfy the demands for portraiture of a portable nature. Miniature painting of portraits had long been in vogue. Indeed, court painters such as Holbein were often sent abroad, commissioned to paint miniatures of prospective royal marriage partners.

Paintings on ivory were unusual. The technique employed watercolours applied with the aid of a magnifying glass in a laborious network of stippled dots and cross-hatched strokes. The completed picture was glazed with a solution of gum arabic and glycerine to bring out the colour and provide a binding protection. A few artists continue the tradition of painting on ivory today.

BIZARRE SUPPORTS

More bizarre painting supports may include the human skin. The art of body painting, both temporary and permanent (tattooing) has been practised since primitive times. The painting of temporary designs on the bodies of nude models is a recent innovation—and an excellent test for anyone contemplating a permanent tattoo. The modern French painter Yves Klein became famous for painting the bodies of his models and directing their movements as they writhed and pressed the wet paint against prepared canvases. Even worms have been dipped in tins of paint and allowed to creep across canvas in the hope that the results may be identifiable as art.

New materials used in modern sculpture have led to a school of painted objects and forms including the human figure. There is a precedent for this in antiquity; polychrome sculpture was painted to resemble living flesh complete with colour-matched eyes and hair.

The most unusual picture support I have encountered is a painting on a spider's web. This small and delicate painting of a madonna and child is hung in Chester City Cathedral, England. The many strands of painted spider's web are sandwiched between two layers of glass. The practice of web painting was primarily a Tyrolean peasant art carried on by a few families for over two centuries. More than one hundred of these rare pictures still exist.

CHAPTER IV

PAPER

History

Writing and drawing surfaces have existed since the beginning of man. Walls of caves were covered with early man's art. The first writing paper was papyrus made from reeds by the Egyptians. Although rough, it was durable, and has preserved records of the Egyptian civilisation. Parchment made from animal skins began to replace papyrus as a writing material.

Paper, in the form we know it today, is a Chinese discovery dating back to the first century AD. The inner bark of the mulberry tree was stripped and the fibres pounded and matted into a sheet. Later, the Chinese pounded rags and hemp to make paper. Mulberry paper is still used for the facing of paintings during restoration. Woodcut artists use it for pulling prints from woodblocks as its light weight and strength permit much hard rubbing.

The Chinese art of papermaking spread to many countries. Papermakers who were captured in battle taught it to the Moors at Samarkand. In the eighth century an industry was established in Baghdad. During the Crusades and the Moorish conquest of North Africa papermaking spread to Europe.

It was not until 1750 that a machine was invented in Holland to break down the rags into fibre. The invention of the printing press by Gutenberg created a large-scale demand for paper.

In 1840 a process was developed for grinding logs into fibrous pulp. Later, it was discovered that wood fibres could be separated if the wood was dissolved in a solution of sulphurous acid. By 1882 woodpulp processing methods were established similar to those employed today.

Handmade Paper

The highly skilled craft of making handmade paper is rapidly becoming a dying art. This is partially due to the deterioration of rags in recent years. Nylon, rubber and numerous other synthetic fibres have replaced much of the pre-war white cotton and linen suitable for making fine paper. Linters, a cotton fibre, are used today.

The advantages of handmade paper over machine or mouldmade paper are its long life and durability. In addition, it is less prone to yellowing. A simple light-proof test may be made by placing one half of a strip of paper into a book, leaving the other half exposed to the sun for two or three weeks. A well-made paper should not show yellowing when the two halves are compared. At one time I used a pure white machinemade paper for etching. A few sheets of this paper were left overlapping each other near a window. When I moved them a few weeks later, the exposed edges were as yellow as egg yolk.

Handmade papers have admirably withstood the test of time. The remarkable condition of paper used by the Old Masters is ample evidence. Handmade paper has in almost every instance outlasted canvas of the same period, perhaps because the Old Master drawings have been kept in a more protected state through the centuries. Some of these drawings, kept under glass or in folios away from dampness and direct sun, are in nearly pristine condition. Their excellent appearance may in some cases be partially due to the attention of a skilled paper restorer. There is little doubt that few would have survived as well had machinemade paper been available to artists at that time.

MAKING HANDMADE PAPER

The technique of making handmade paper is exacting and time-consuming. Each sheet is made individually, which gives the irregular texture prized by watercolour painters. A good handmade paper requires about three months to make, allowing for maturation. The price charged is understandable when one learns something of the process involved. A detailed account is described in *Papermaking by Hand* by J. Barcham Green, whose family has been engaged in papermaking since the end of the seventeenth century.

After the paper has been beaten, pulped, passed through the vat house, pressed, dried, sized and matured, it is ready for finishing. It is sorted into three grades: Good, Sorts, and Bad Broken. The Good is tied into reams ready for sale. Manufacturers can produce only about seventy-five per cent of Good. The Sorts are divided into Retree (slightly defective) and Outsides (definitely defective). Retree and Outsides are sold separately at a reduction in price. Art students find them a good buy. Prices are generally less for a quire (25 sheets) than the individual sheet. A considerable saving can be made in purchasing a ream (500 sheets).

A handmade paper may be recognized by its deckled irregular edges and usually the manufacturers' incorporated watermark. It is sometimes dated with the year it was made. The 'right' side of the paper to be used can be ascertained by the readability of these watermarks and dates.

HANDMADE PAPER FOR ETCHING
Unlike the other printmaking processes, etching requires that the paper be dampened beforehand. When the paper is impressed into the plate, it is in an expanded condition. Upon drying, the paper shrinks to less than its original dimensions. There can be a difference of up to one half inch in the size of the impressed print and the plate from which it was made.

Quite often the quality of the handmade paper will differ between batches. I have even found the dimensions varying up to a half inch, which can be disconcerting. Despite these drawbacks the artist is amply compensated by the knowledge that his work is on the best quality paper available.

One of the finest handmade papermakers has unfortunately ceased production, much to my personal distress as I had begun printing the editions of several etching plates on their paper. I was ultimately forced to complete the editions with another paper. Whenever possible I now buy a sufficient supply of paper to complete an edition. I seldom use a paper manufactured expressly for etching because I find they are not as suitable for my purposes as some of the watercolour and drawing papers.

Mouldmade and Machinemade Paper

The growing scarcity of handmade paper has led many artists to employ mouldmade paper as a substitute. It is a paper of good quality with a method of production both faster and cheaper than handmade.

The manufacture of mouldmade paper involves the preparation of several sheets at one time in moulds operated by machine instead of by hand. This gives the paper a more uniform texture.

The paper produced by machine process is cut into sheets from continuous rolls. These are imprinted with a mechanical grain. Most of the cheaper papers are made this way. Many are quite suitable for prints, watercolours or drawings, but their life expectancy may be short. Sizing substances such as starch, alum, rosin and clay may be added to the pulp blends. Coloured fibres are produced by the addition of dyes.

Newsprint is a blend of one part sulfite pulp and three parts of ground wood with little refining. The acidity content of newsprint is high. It yellows quickly, and without attention will decompose in time.

SIZES AND SURFACES

Artists' papers are catalogued by art suppliers according to their usage, size, weight and surface. A paper described as seventy-two pounds refers to the weight of one ream, which is 500 sheets. Therefore, a paper of one hundred forty pounds is thicker. Some variation in exact dimensions may appear between papers of different manufacture. For instance, one Imperial sheet may be $30\frac{1}{2}'' \times 22\frac{1}{2}''$ and another $30'' \times 22''$. The possibility of variation should be considered when preparing mounts or buying Imperial port-folios, which are sometimes cut to fit the smaller dimension.

In the trade, specific names are given to paper dimensions as listed:

	Size in Inches
Antiquarian	53×31
Double Elephant	40×27
Imperial	$31\frac{1}{2} \times 22\frac{1}{2}$
Royal	$24 \times 19\frac{1}{2}$
Medium	$22 \times 17\frac{1}{2}$
Demy	$20 \times 15\frac{1}{2}$

There are three described surfaces: Rough, Not and Hot-pressed. Rough shows the grain of the felt; Not, a medium surfaced paper, is pressed wet into the pack press giving an eggshell finish; HP (hot-pressed), a smooth paper, is glazed between zinc plates and passed through rollers under heavy pressure. Hot-pressed papers are generally less absorbent. Despite its name, heat is no longer applied in the process.

The amount of gelatine size contained in the paper will vary. Some papers, in order to be suitable for etching or watercolour washes, must be soaked overnight and lightly sponged to remove excess size. Waterleaf is an unsized paper which is sometimes slightly less expensive. It is highly absorbent and should be handled carefully while damp.

Art paper is made for innumerable purposes, from clay-surfaced papers prepared for silver point drawings to oil-sketching paper for painting. The surface of the drawing paper can be affected greatly by the support used while drawing. A rough textured drawing can be done on a smooth surfaced paper by placing a heavily textured paper beneath. The opposite effect can be obtained with layers of newsprint placed beneath a rough surface.

The Paper Restorer

Ours is an age of specialization, and the field of restoration is no exception. The paper restorer is an expert whose work requires patience, skill and attention to detail. A great advantage paper restorers have over painting restorers is that they can more easily receive work by post from anywhere in the world. Experts in Britain and the USA receive a great deal of work from countries without trained personnel or facilities.

A restorer in charge of a collection of prints and drawings in a museum or public archive is responsible for their overall maintenance and display. His duties are akin to those of the painting restorer.

Examination

A glass top table, illuminated by a light underneath, is advantageous for the examination of paper damage and watermarks. The paper is carefully examined to determine the course of treatment. If the paper is hard or brittle to the touch, the slightest disturbance when immersed may cause tearing. This condition frequently occurs in paper exposed to tropical climates or paper with a high acidity factor. Soft spongy papers also present a problem and are not immersed as the glue or gelatine size will inevitably weaken in the solution, rendering the paper weak and liable to tear.

Observations are made of any creases, tears, unusual stains and the likely effect of bleaching agents on ink or colours. Signatures and writing added to the art may be fugitive and appropriate protection must be given them.

Paper is a hygroscopic (moisture absorbing) material. The moisture in turn promotes growth of tiny micro-organisms which attack the size and encourage mould to form. Sometimes a group of rust brown spots appear, due to micro-organisms forming on iron salts in the paper. This condition is described as *foxing*. Many prints requiring cleaning suffer from these conditions.

Removing Supports

Paper or light cardboard backing are detached from a print by being soaked in lukewarm water with the print surface face up. Separation should take place in the water. In the case of starchpaste so firmly fixed that it does not respond to this treatment, the addition of an enzyme may be used to act upon the paste. Heavy paper backing is softened quickly with a few drops of lissapol, a wetting agent, in the water. Heavy cardboard backing is removed by inserting a long flat bone paperknife at one corner and removing the laminated layers separately. Before reaching the last layer, it may be necessary to hold the print card-side down over a steaming kettle until the card becomes pliable. It is then laid face down on blotting paper and the softened card is removed. Some compositions of cardboard may require rubbing away with the fingertips while wet. The card must always be removed from the print, not the print from the card. No attempt is made to separate the print and card by pulling them apart at the corners.

Canvas backing has been given to many old prints. They are usually fixed on to a wooden stretcher frame. The edges of the canvas are slit and it is removed from the stretcher. The print, with attached canvas, is laid face down on clean blotting paper. The back of the canvas is sponged with water containing lissapol, allowing time for the water to penetrate the adhesive. The canvas is turned print side up and one corner of the print is separated and gradually pulled back towards the diagonal corner with a slight side to side motion. If any signs of tearing of the paper occur during the removal operation, work is stopped and the canvas resoaked to allow the solution time to soften the adhesive before resumption.

Wood backing has been responsible for serious damage to paper. In the past pine and other highly acid resinous woods were used for backing. Resinous exudes, causing discolouration and brittleness, often repeat the wood grain even to knot holes appearing on the paper surface. Unfortunately prints, drawings and watercolours are still being adhered to wooden supports in some frameshops. The composition boards of today, however, are less likely to be injurious to the paper. The removal of a wood backing is laborious if the drawing or print is attached with glue or is not immersable. The removal is effected in a similar manner to an oil panel transfer. The wood must be cut away from the back and pared with a scalpel to within a fraction of the paper. If the work is immersable, soaking in warm water with lissapol should soon detach it from the remaining board.

Surface Cleaning

Dust and dirt should be dry cleaned from the surface before the paper is immersed to avoid it becoming ingrained in the paper. This is accomplished either by a draft clean powder, used for drafting and architectural drawings, or with finely crumbled art gum, replenished at intervals during the cleaning. A soft cloth is used in a delicate circular movement to rotate the dirt-collecting particles over the area. This method should not be used for unfixed pencil or chalk drawings but dirt and finger smudges around the borders may be removed safely. In some cases the dry treatment may be all that is necessary. Immersing paper even in mild chemicals should be avoided when dry cleaning will suffice. Cellulose fibres are affected to some degree by all bleaching. Ingrained dirt which cannot be removed with this dry cleaning method may be sometimes traced to an earlier bleaching without previous dry cleaning.

A cuttlefish bone is an excellent abrasive for removing spots. It can take the print off a newspaper without wearing through the newsprint.

CAUTIONS

Caution is the keynote of every restorer's procedure when using bleaching agents. If toxic substances are to be used, sufficient ventilation is essential. Papers which appear thin and fragile or fugitive in colour or ink are not immersed. Prints and drawings made with carbon ink or pencil can be placed in a mild bleach with reasonable safety. The restorer may start with the mildest solution and test a corner before immersing the entire work. Careful rinsing must follow all bleaching operations to disperse the chemicals from the paper. Lifting a wet print by the corners should be avoided.

Cleaning by Immersion

A print should be placed in slowly circulating cold water in preparation for a bleaching bath. In some instances a thorough rinsing in water alone will clean light mildew stains and marks, giving the print a fresh appearance. Further general cleaning may be carried out with a mild soft soap. The wet print is laid face down on glass and wet soapy foam is applied gently with a large soft brush to the back of the print. If the paper surface remains intact the print is reversed and the front similarly lathered. Rinsing in clear water must be prolonged to ensure complete removal of the soap.

The wet paper is not lifted by hand, but is transported in and out of the tray on a sheet of glass or perspex. Although appearing heavy and strong, some papers become like tissue when wet and the precaution of using a support must be taken. The floating print adheres to the support when it is raised from the tray and can be turned over for transferring without fear of detachment. Extra large prints which do not fit into trays are treated in a sink or even a bathtub. A support of sufficient size can be made by cutting a section from a polythene clothes bag. When an oversize print is ready for removal, the thin polythene is manipulated under the print to which it clings when raised.

Another method of preparing a bath for an oversized print is to place four boards together (like a frame without nails), standing on edge, to form the sides of a tray. A sheet of polythene is draped over the temporary tray and the solution is poured into it.

Bleaching

The simplest form of bleaching may be accomplished by exposure to the sun and air. The arid atmosphere of Middle Eastern deserts has preserved ancient scrolls and writings that could not have survived elsewhere in different climatic conditions.

The object of bleaching by immersion is to break down a stain into colourless matter. The greatest danger lies in the process being carried too far. Papers which are left too long in a bleaching solution present a bone-white and chalky appearance due to the deterioration of the fibres. Inks, lead pencil and pigments will suffer considerable loss of brilliance. Fortunately however most etchings and engravings are printed with carbon ink, which is relatively insoluble in bleaching solutions.

The print is kept under close surveillance during this chemical action so that it can be removed before overbleaching occurs. Afterwards, thorough rinsing in circulating clear water must be carried out to remove all traces of the chemical. The water is kept circulating slowly in the sink for about two or three hours.

Fugitive coloured papers, watercolours, pastels, chalk drawings and ink washes must not be immersed. Descriptions of methods of treatment for these works are given in the pages following.

Bleaches for paper restoration are obtainable through chemists, drug houses or industrial chemical companies. A more comprehensive, technical examination of bleaches and works on paper is found in Dr H. J. Plender-leith's erudite book *The Conservation of Antiquities and Works of Art*.

THREE PRINCIPAL BLEACHES AND THEIR USES

SODIUM HYPOCHLORITE

Sometimes called *chlorinated soda*, sodium hypochlorite can be purchased in one-gallon winchester bottles. It should be a commercial mixture marked '10% W/V available chlorine'. This solution should be kept tightly stoppered in a cool and dark space or it will soon lose strength. It is the most generally used bleach for the removal of foxing, mildew and discolouration stains. The bleaching bath is prepared with approximately one half cup of sodium hypochlorite to two quarts of water. Several prints may be bleached in the same solution, provided the water does not become discoloured. The tray containing the print is rocked gently to and fro at intervals to agitate the sodium hypochlorite. The stains will lighten and gradually disappear. The print is removed as soon as the last trace of discolouration has dissolved. After a quick rinsing in water, it is then transferred to a previously prepared bath of one teaspoon of sodium thiosulphate crystals mixed in one quart of warm water, which arrests the action of the bleach. Sodium thiosulphate is also used in photographic studios for the fixing of photographic prints. The print is left in the sodium thiosulphate bath several minutes before being removed for thorough washing.

SODIUM CHLORITE (Chlorine Dioxide Gas Bleach)

The dry usage of this bleaching agent necessitates specialized laboratory equipment. The dry method releases a yellow chlorine dioxide gas from the sodium chlorite solution. The gas produced is the bleaching agent rather than the crystals. A specially constructed gas chamber is necessary for its use. Fragile paper or drawings in chalk which cannot be immersed are most suited to being treated by gas although certain colour pigments may be affected.

Alternatively, either of two wet methods are advocated for using sodium chlorite. The first, chlorine dioxide in water, also involves some specialized equipment. It is mainly applicable to prints and drawings which can remain only a short time in water. The second method, sodium chlorite-formaldehyde bleach, is perhaps the most commonly used solution for firmly set pencil drawings and prints of carbon ink composition.

When the sodium chlorite-formaldehyde bleach is used, a fume hood or another form of ventilation by extraction is a necessity. Without this facility, the bleaching treatment may be staged in the open air. The bleaching formula is approximately one teaspoon of technical sodium chlorite for every quart of water. The bath tray is filled to the desired level and a few drops of thirty-seven per cent formaldehyde or topane are added. The solution quickly turns yellow from the release of chlorine dioxide. About twenty minutes of bleaching in this solution will rid the paper of stains and foxing, although more persistent stains may require a longer period of immersion. The bath may be used for three or four prints, but they must be treated consecutively as the solution cannot be used effectively after storage.

Sodium chlorite is one of the safest bleaching solutions for paper. It produces no chlorination of cellulose fibres that is damaging to paper structure. A litmus paper may be used to test for evidence of chloride after sodium hypochlorite or sodium chlorite bleaching. When rinsing is complete the print is placed in a tray filled with fresh water. A litmus test paper is dipped in the water. If it turns blue it is positive, indicating that further washing is necessary to remove the residue.

An authoritative article on *The Bleaching of Stained and Discoloured Pictures on Paper with Sodium Chlorite and Chlorine Dioxide* by Rutherford J. Gettens appeared in the UNESCO publication *Museum*, volume I, no 2 1952.

CHLORAMINE-T

One of the mildest bleaching agents, chloramine-T, is suitable for delicate watercolours, chalk drawings and fugitive ink washes. Rinsing in water is not required as it does not leave behind any detrimental residue.

Chloramine-T is prepared by mixing one teaspoon of crystals to one quart of warm water. The solution is stirred until dissolved and applied directly to the stain with a brush. A piece or blotting paper is used to cover the dampened stain and a sheet of glass is placed on top. Repeated applications may be required to effect bleaching.

Prints and drawings on fragile paper respond favourably to chloramine-T lightly sprayed with an atomizer on the reverse side. The print is covered with blotting paper and placed under glass, followed by repeated applications until the stains on the front have disappeared. Chloramine-T may also be used for immersable papers in a bleaching bath by adding one teaspoon of crystals to each quart of warm water as required. The bleaching action is comparatively slow. The print may be removed from the bath for close observation, then reimmersed until the stains are no longer visible.

OTHER BLEACHES AND INDIVIDUAL STAIN REMOVERS

OXIDIZED WHITE AND RED LEAD AND FLY MARKS (*Hydrogen Peroxide*)
Equal volumes of hydrogen peroxide and ordinary ether are shaken together in a bottle. The layer of ether rises to the top as the hydrogen peroxide containing less desirable elements settles visibly to the bottom. Sufficient pure hydrogen peroxide is dispersed in the clear etherial layer to effect bleaching. A small sable brush or swab is dipped into the clear layer only and the solution is stippled on to the affected area with repeated applications.

A small piece of plaster of Paris impregnated with hydrogen peroxide can be suspended over the stain to be treated without actually touching the paper. The vapours will act to remove the oxidization.

COFFEE AND TEA STAINS (*Potassium Perborate*)
Two or three drops of potassium perborate are mixed in two-thirds cup of water and stippled with a brush on to the previously water-dampened stain. When the solution begins to dry, stippling is repeated until most of the stain is removed. A final bleach with chloramine-T should remove the last traces.

GREASE, OIL AND TAR STAINS (*Pyridine*)
The stain is first scraped with a knife to remove any particles still on the surface. It is then treated with a concentrated solution of pyridine as many times as needed. Solvents such as benzene, white spirit and ethyl acetate are among several possible cleaners. Pyridine is toxic and must be used with caution.

GREASE AND WAX STAINS (*Petrol*)
The wax deposit is scraped with a knife. After testing, the print is totally immersed in a petrol bath and the stain area is brushed until clean. Thorough washing to remove the petrol is mandatory. Some local absorption of a grease stain can be effected by applying a detergent soap powder to the water-dampened spot, should the print not be immersable in petrol.

BLOOD, SAUCES, ETC. (*Enzymes*)
Organic substances known as enzymes can render some organic stains soluble through digestion. The application of enzymes to stains on paper is still in the experimental stage. Commercial digester powder preparations

for clothing and textiles are already on the retail market. Enzymes in the digestive system of our bodies are instrumental in the breakdown of proteins, fats and sugars.

INK AND IRON STAINS (*Sodium Formaldehyde Sulphoxylate*)
Several courses of treatment are possible for ink stains. The most effective treatment is placing sodium formaldehyde sulphoxylate powder directly on the dampened stain. A very thorough washing must follow.

PROTECTING INK SIGNATURES
Often prints are signed or contain writing in iron gall inks which will dissolve in bleach. A nitrocellulose film painted over these will protect them during bleaching. Two or three drops of celluloid five per cent in a solvent of equal amounts of amyl acetate and acetone comprise the solution.

Varnish Removal

The varnishing of prints, particularly coloured sporting and hunting scenes, has been popular since the last century. One look at an old varnished print that has turned the colour of mahogany should do much to stop this practice among picture framers. To be fair, it is not entirely their fault. Clients bothered by glass reflections encourage this practice and manufacturers produce spray tins of varnish that they claim to be suitable for paper. Their claims seem reasonable until the varnish begins to deteriorate. A perfect non-yellowing, non-cracking varnish has yet to be invented. Varnish leaves a deeply embedded stain in the fabric of the paper unlike varnish over an oil paint surface.

The degree of difficulty in removing varnish from paper depends upon the type of varnish that has been used and the condition of the paper. The main types of prints encountered requiring this treatment are coloured engravings and mezzotints. In nearly all attempts at varnish removal, the underlying colours will be affected, particularly if they are handpainted with watercolour or oils rather than printer's inks. Despite this problem, the print will appear so immensely improved that the loss of some colour will seem negligible.

Every print requires individual treatment so that no one method can be advised. Sometimes the varnish on a print may resemble old brown leather which is seemingly irremoveable. A varnished print in this state of deterioration can be successfully restored. For example, the print may be treated with the following method: After initial cleaning, the print is immersed in industrial methylated spirit (alcohol) and gently rubbed with cotton wool to dissolve the hardened varnish. It is removed from the alcohol and placed in a bath of ammonia and water in about one to ten proportions to force the remaining varnish from the paper. The print is then transferred to a bath of acetic acid and water in one to twenty proportions to remove the residue stain. The latter entails quick dipping, removal and inspection three successive times. Afterwards, repeated applications of chloramine-T complete the operation. Following treatment for acidity, the print is dried, pressed and mounted.

Acidity and Treatment

Many papers acquire a high acid content during manufacture through the introduction of alum and the residue of chemical bleaching. Other papers acidify in the process of ageing, an action which continues unless treated. Recognition of this acidulous condition in paper is by sight or touch. Advanced cases are usually brown in colour and brittle. Laboratories employ an instrument known as a PH Meter to make an accurate test of the amount of acid present in paper. The PH Meter is used primarily for medical purposes, an example of adapting other scientific equipment to the field of art conservation.

Magnesium carbonate, the chalk used by gymnasts, is adapted to the treatment of acidity. One half teaspoon of the powder is mixed into one quart of distilled water and poured into a seltzer cylinder. A carbon dioxide cartridge is discharged converting the solution to magnesium bicarbonate. It is agitated and left to stand for half an hour and agitated again before being sprayed on to the paper. The paper is allowed to dry between each application. Three or four applications should be sufficient to reduce the acidity. The solution will keep for several weeks.

The amount of acidity in the paper should be tested with the PH Meter. Readings taken after treatment show almost complete neutralization of the paper. Even if a PH Meter is not available, there is still satisfaction in knowing an effective step has been taken towards reducing the acidity content of the paper. An avant garde fine art magazine decided to devote an issue to self-destructive art. The paper edition was designed to destroy itself eventually by the use of paper with a very high acidity factor. One leading museum subsequently declined to accept the magazine for their collection on the grounds that it might contaminate the archives.

POTASSIUM PERMANGANATE FOR BLEACHING WOODPULP
Papers with a high acidity content such as newsprint, woodpulp drawing paper and prints with wood-resin exude stains respond well to treatment in potassium permanganate, a purple-red crystalline salt. One teaspoonful of the crystals is dissolved in three quarts of water in one tray and one teaspoonful of citric acid is added to three quarts of water in another. After immersion in water, the print is placed into the tray containing potassium permanganate. The paper turns pink from the absorption of the purple permanganate bleach and the coloured cloudiness may make observation of the print somewhat difficult. The print restorer must rely on his experience to judge the length of time required for proper bleaching. When the stains have disappeared the print is returned for a brief fresh-water rinse. It is reimmersed in the citric acid bath until the pink tinge disperses. Following the potassium permanganate bleaching, the paper should be treated for acidity by the magnesium bicarbonate method. Potassium permanganate has properties detrimental to the paper's structure and is not advisable for bleaching other papers.

Resizing Papers

Paper demonstrating brittleness or soft absorbent limpness can be strengthened by resizing. A sheet of gelatine is dissolved in a bath of warm water in which the print is immersed. After thorough penetration, heavy papers may be hung on a line to dry. Light or fragile papers are treated without immersion by brushing the size through tissue on to the dampened paper.

Some papers, when soaked, present a blotchy look with semi-transparent areas. These are the result of micro-organisms attacking the size. In order to resize the paper, it must first be soaked in a bath of warm water until most of the old size is dispersed. After rinsing in clear water, it is ready to be resized.

Discretion must be exercised when drying wet paper. One preoccupied restorer, looking for a place to set a prized print, laid it on a metal table to dry overnight. The next day he found it had turned rust red!

Eradicating Folds and Creases

Many prints have been thoughtlessly folded or accidentally creased. To treat this condition the dampened print is placed face down on glass, pressed by hand with blotting paper and left to dry. If the creases are not too severe they will be permanently smoothed as the paper dries and shrinks. The crease may be further alleviated by continued pressing under weights.

Minor creases in a damp print can be ironed out with a warm iron passed steadily over a protecting cloth to ensure the paper is not scorched. More severe creases must be stretched and held with the method described in the section *Backing Prints*, pages 78-9. Filling with cellulose powder and toning are sometimes necessary to match the torn fibres in a deep crease.

Mending Tears and Strengthening

Small tears in prints can be joined while damp. A piece of thin mulberry paper is ripped in the shape of the tear but large enough to overlap about one half inch. Paste is applied to the back of the tear and the mulberry paper is pressed into place.

Paper with large tears, numerous small tears, or of weak substance can be strengthened and tears joined if the back of the print is adhered to a sheet of medium or heavy mulberry tissue of equal size.

Patching and Filling

Prints are often encountered with torn corners, small wormholes or gaping holes and missing sections. The paper restorer should continually collect samples of various types of paper, no matter how small, for use in patching. Bits of lithography, mezzotint, stippling, engraved line and aquatint should all be retained. One day they may prove suitable to replace missing areas in prints of the same technique.

Repairing holes or sections outside the actual drawn or printed area is not as difficult a task as patching within the design itself. To repair the missing segment, a paper of similar tone and texture is chosen. Tea and coffee can be used as staining agents to tone the paper patch to a close proximity of the original. The patch should be cut about one-eighth inch larger than the area of the missing piece to allow for chamfering the overlap. Chamfering means to bevel or make a sloping edge. A scalpel blade, held sideways, is used to scrape the paper thin. The back edges of the hole are chamfered similarly and thinly pasted. The chamfered edges of the patch are coated with a small amount of paste and joined to the edges of the hole at the back. The patch is then ready for pressing to blend it invisibly with the surface of the print.

Patches are normally applied to large holes and tears with missing fragments. Holes up to a new penny in size can be filled with paper pulp. The pulp is prepared by chamfering unsized paper of similar structure until a little pile of fuzz is collected. The paper fuzz is placed into a bottle containing sufficient distilled water to form the torn fibres into a gelatinous mass. It is allowed to stand for a few hours then stirred and mashed. The pulp is then removed and laid over the hole at the back. The pulp fibres are teased out to link with the edges of the hole and any excess water is blotted away. A dab of paste and mulberry tissue is adhered to the back of the print to ensure the pulp is kept in place. It is then ready for pressing.

Some paper restoration laboratories employ a device with rotating metal blades, much like a food blender, to produce an instant fibrous cotton wool which can then be made into pulp when needed.

Cellulose powder has been used to fill small holes and cracks. It is mixed with the adhesive sodium carboxymethyl cellulose, called Cellofas B, and distilled water. The cellulose powder can be toned with watercolour or tea before being applied with a spatula. The paste is worked into cracks or deep folds and spread thinly beyond the edges to fill any surrounding worn area. Unless the print has previously been backed, mulberry tissue is placed on the reverse side when the holes are filled.

Missing corners are replaced by overlaying the torn sheet on to a selected patch paper, preferably a salvaged corner, and traced. The new section should overlap the torn edge of the print by one quarter of an inch. The patch paper overlap is chamfered on top while the torn print edge is chamfered on the reverse. The two are joined and held in place with a strip of mulberry tissue pasted on the reverse, torn to follow the direction of the tear. The repaired print should be mounted to prevent handling.

Backing Prints

Works on paper of little intrinsic value may be backed with a paper or card of greater dimension. The backing permits handling of the work without danger of finger marks or tears. Cardboard mounting will, however, add to their weight and the space required for storage in drawers or portfolios. A thermoplastic or dry mounting tissue may be purchased in photographic supply shops for mounting works of lesser quality. They may be ironed on to supports easily, the thermoplastic tissue melting to create a bond.

One way of backing a print is to paste it on to a sheet of paper and stretch it on a board support. To accomplish this, the print is laid face down on a polythene sheet and dampened. A wheat paste, composed of wheat flour and water with a few drops of formaldehyde, to discourage mould growth, is brushed on the back. The polythene and print are then turned over on to a previously dampened backing paper of good quality. The transparency of the polythene permits a clear view of the print for centring. The polythene is then pulled away and the print blotted.

When the print and backing paper have dried short of cockling, a gummed paper tape one or two inches wide is wet and adhered to the edges of the backing paper and to a rigid support. As the paper slowly dries, it tightens and may split if it is allowed to remain too long. To alleviate the stress, the tape is slit at the paper's edge. Only the top and one side need be released to relieve the tension. The two edges are retaped. It should be safe to leave indefinitely, but if signs of further stress occur the edges are slit again. Ideally the paper tape should be weaker than the paper backing so that if splitting does occur it will be in the tape rather than the print.

A backing method used by libraries involves sizing, stretching and laying prints and documents in a single operation. A sheet of terylene (shirt quality) is wrapped tightly to enclose a substantial perspex sheet previously coated with Cellofas B. The grains are mixed thoroughly in distilled water and allowed to stand for half an hour before using. It must form a brushable gel. The Cellofas B is applied with a large brush or sponge in smooth liberal coats on both front and back of the terylene. A damp sheet of paper for backing is laid and centred on the terylene. Cellofas B is brushed over the front. The damp print is laid face down on a thin polythene sheet which is then turned face up to lay and centre on the newly adhered backing paper. The polythene is removed and blotting paper pressed from the centre outwards to eliminate air bubbles and remove excess Cellofas B. The perspex support can be stood vertically. The print is left to dry for about forty-eight hours and then removed by undoing the terylene, removing the perspex and separating the backing. If required the backed print can be pressed. Sodium carboxymethyl cellulose is completely non-acid, sterile and invisible when dry. Moreover, it simultaneously sizes the paper by increasing its cellulose content.

FLATTENING PAPER
A screw-type block printing press is an asset when a quantity of work is to be flattened. Without this apparatus blotting paper, waxed paper, blankets, drawing boards and weights will suffice.

A more rapid method of flattening and drying work is by blotting excess moisture from the print, placing it between dry blotters and sandwiching it between two sheets of plate glass. The blotters are replaced at intervals to allow maximum moisture absorption.

Cleaning and Restoring of Particular Works

PARCHMENT

Parchment requires special attention because, although it can resemble paper, it is an animal skin.

More than one restorer has, in early days, accidentally treated a work on parchment along with other works on paper. Immersing parchment in water for treatment can result in shrinking the works to half their original size.

PASTELS AND CHALK DRAWINGS

The great disadvantage of pastel as a medium is the fragility of the powder colour. Ideally, fixative solutions should not be sprayed on to the pastel, since the important last touches, overall tone and highlights are either blown away or considerably reduced in brilliance. If a fixative is used it should be sprayed up and over the pastel to settle in a fine film on the surface. Pastels should be protected by framing as soon as possible, although even pastels framed behind glass are vulnerable to pigment loss. A sudden knock can detach pigment particles. Pastels must never be permitted to touch the glass or the powder will transfer. To avoid this happening, a thick mount board must be used or small wedges inserted at the edges between the glass and the mount.

Mould growth may appear on the paper size, pigments and the gum tragacanth binding medium. This must be picked off with a small brush dipped in alcohol, followed by thymol sterilization of the picture.

Very old pastels and chalk drawings may become firmly fixed in the paper as the gum becomes bound to it. Stains on these drawings can be treated by chloramine-T spray applications. If the chalk is stable, light spraying can take place on the surface. If the drawing might be affected, it can be sprayed on the back.

WATERCOLOURS

Watercolour pigments are unsafe to wet unless they are at least twenty-five years old. Even then many colours may prove fugitive. Stains are best treated with the described chloramine-T methods. Retouching or compensation in colour areas lost through bad staining or damage should be carried out with full regard to the artist's original intention.

INDIAN MINIATURES

A frequent condition affecting Indian miniature paintings is the blackening of the white and red lead pigments. The ethereal hydrogen peroxide solution, as already described, should restore the original colours. If the blackening remains, the original paint was probably metallic silver, for which there is no satisfactory method of treatment.

Flaking of the paint layers is quite common in miniatures because the binding of the water soluble paint to the paper is somewhat fragile. A powder called 'soluble nylon' can be used to correct this condition. It is mixed with industrial methylated spirit to form a transparent adhesive which is carefully applied to the underside of the flakes with a small brush. Soluble nylon is a thermoplastic material and the laying of flaking fragments is accomplished with an electrically heated spatula. Retouching is carried out in watercolours.

JAPANESE PRINTS

The mulberry paper used for Japanese prints is very durable in its dry state. Because it becomes soft when wet, it is generally unsuitable for immersion treatment. Fortunately foxing and mildew do not form easily on mulberry paper. Stains will generally respond to chloramine-T spray or brushing through tissue. Some of the pigments used in Japanese printmaking are fugitive and tests should be made on colours such as mauve to determine the amount of wetting they can stand before bleeding.

Lamination of Documents

Documents can be strengthened and protected by lamination. A process devised in America in the 1930s by W. J. Barrow is the most commonly used. First the paper is given a deacidification treatment and then placed between two sheets of cellulose acetate and an outer layer of tissue. Placed in the Barrow laminator, it is heated and passed through two calendar rollers under pressure to melt the cellulose acetate. The tissue blends into the pressure-formed layers. The document is rigidly protected on both sides and any writing is left clearly visible. The lamination film may, after many years, begin to yellow and become brittle. It may then be dissolved in a chemical bath and replaced. A description of the process is found in

W. J. Barrow's *Procedures and Equipment Used in the Barrow Method of Restoring Manuscripts and Documents.*

Fumigation

Early mould growth can be sterilized in a prepared chamber. This treatment is particularly suitable for books and fragile art work on paper that will not withstand bleaching.

Any unpainted, air-tight cupboard of sufficient size to accommodate the fungus-infected objects can be used. A forty watt electric lamp is placed at the bottom of the cupboard. A quarter teaspoon of thymol crystals in an enamel plate is placed two inches above the lamp. The books are opened and stood on end to allow the vapours free access to the pages. The heat from the lamp, when switched on, melts the crystals, releasing a thymol vapour. Dampness and the musty smell will disperse readily if the lamp is employed about three or four hours each day for a week. This sterilization treatment is not suitable for oil paintings because the paint films tend to soften.

Another method of sterilization is to release formaldehyde vapours. A dish containing forty per cent formaldehyde is placed beneath the paper in a sealed box or cupboard and left for a day.

Selecting and Cutting a Mount

Once the processes of restoration are completed, a mount should be cut to protect the print. It would be unwise to invite a recurrence of the conditions that originally caused the deterioration, yet some framers still use inferior materials. Expensive gilt, hand-carved frames and linen-covered mounts embellish the exterior, while underneath the print is exposed to dangers such as contamination from acid pulp backing, yellowing tape or unsuitable adhesives. These will ultimately lead to discolouration and mould growth.

Ideally, mounts and backing should be one hundred per cent rag board with linen hinges and neutral soluble paste. Unfortunately, rag board of quality is becoming scarce. Any cardboard used to secure the mount in a frame should be thymol impregnated. An inert paper tape should be used to enclose the back of the frame to prevent dust from entering.

Skilful mount cutting takes practice. A poorly cut bevel or a slip of the knife at a corner cannot be hidden. The tools required are a knife designed for mount cutting, an oilstone, a heavy metal straight edge, a set square, and an extra cardboard on which to cut.

There are several ways of measuring the aperture to fit the picture. The simplest procedure is to measure the horizontal dimension of the picture. Let us suppose this is twenty-four inches. Then measure the mount card. Let us assume this is thirty inches. The centre of the card, being fifteen inches, is marked in pencil. The picture measurement is halved, making twelve inches. A line is drawn twelve inches on either side of the card centre mark. This will establish identical measurements of the sides, which in this case are three inches. The vertical measurements can vary slightly according to taste. Generally the top is the same width as the sides. The bottom should be a minimum of one-half inch wider than the top to create an optical illusion. A picture placed in the exact centre of a mount gives the impression of being too low. Faint pencil lines are drawn with a T-square to intersect at the four corners as a cutting guide.

The cutting of the mount requires an extremely sharp knife. An extra card is laid beneath the mount to protect the table. The metal straight edge is placed just outside the pencil line. The knife is held at a forty-five degree angle against the straight edge and cut with a steady pressure towards the operator. The straight edge must be kept in place and the cut repeated in long, sure strokes until it is through the mount. Attention must be paid not to cut past the intersecting corner lines. A small pinhole at each corner is a helpful guide. Any fraying of the mount corners can be removed with a razor blade.

TYPES OF MOUNTS

GUARDED
Guarding, the simplest of all mounts, utilizes a single sheet of card. The print is held to the card by four strips of paper placed at the edge along the length and width of the print. The strips are folded over lengthwise and pasted to the board, folded side inward. Paste is then applied to the exposed strip halves and the print placed on top, ready for pressing. Guarding is quick and requires little storage space. The margins of the paper are left exposed. The print is not fully protected from tearing unless a hinged, window overthrow mount is added. A guarded mount is normally recommended for works of little value or importance.

OVERTHROW
The commonly used overthrow mount permits lifting from either the side

or the bottom for inspection of the print margins. A window opening is cut to fit the print from a card mount and the mount is then hinged with linen tape at one edge of a backboard. The print is hinged with two linen tabs to the backboard so that it aligns with the window aperture.

INLAID

A handsome presentation is achieved by inlay mounting. A window, one-eighth inch smaller than the drawing at each edge, is cut from hand-made paper. The window edges are then chamfered and the paper is adhered to a backing board. The reverse edges of the drawing may be very lightly chamfered. Both drawing and window edges are pasted and the drawing placed on top. It is then put under pressure. The edges of the drawing are pressed into the chamfer and blend invisibly with the mount. This provides a lightweight mount showing the borders of the drawing without danger of catching and tearing. A window mount may be added if desired.

SPECIAL MOUNTS

Mounts of dubious quality may be made more longlasting by being covered with linen obtainable in varied tones and textures. The added cost is compensated for by their continued unmarred appearance. Many cardboard mounts, framed and under glass, are spotted from oxidization of the iron impurities in the poor quality cardboard. The use of textured linen makes less obvious the inevitable wood splinters or small bits of card that may wedge between the mount and the glass. These appear most unsightly on ordinary white mounts.

Watercolour mounts may be further enhanced by wash borders. Spacing is arbitrary. Any combination of lines, tones and colours in keeping with the picture may be used. A ruling pen and flat brushes are needed to embellish the wash borders. Gold and silver paper can be cut in strips with a knife and straight edge. These may be used in place of the wash lines, and are stuck down with spirit gum or paste.

Storage

Art museums and libraries must house and care for large collections of art and documents on paper. Prints, drawings and watercolours are generally kept in drawers or in special cases on shelves. Various substances are placed inside to absorb moisture. These include anhydrous calcium chloride, silica gel and kaken gel. Silica gel, frequently used in packing articles such as paint brushes and transistors, is perhaps the most familiar. To ensure the prolonged life of art on paper, full restoration treatment must be completed and proper mounting materials used throughout before storage. Works in tropical climates require special consideration and facilities.

Storage arrangements in museums and libraries are continually being examined and improved. Inadequate storage planning may result in paper being exposed to deleterious elements. In the home, some thought should be given to the relative safety and conditions of the space allotted for storage. It should be dry and accessible. Paper should not be stored in a basement where rising dampness will propagate mould growth or near water pipes which might burst. If the works are wrapped for storing some small packets of silica gel should be included. At no time should paper be left in the proximity of substances affected by mould or foxing. Works stored for long periods should be inspected regularly for silverfish and other insects prone to paper habitations.

CHAPTER V

PAINTING MEDIA AND TECHNIQUE

Traditional Media

Looking at paintings has occupied man since the cave dwellers first drew their magical hunting symbols on rough stone walls. Artists throughout the ages have tried to communicate their individual ways of thinking, seeing and recording visual or imagined images. Religion, superstition, politics, war, joy and grief — all the expressions of the human condition have been depicted in the work of the artist.

Each generation views works of art with varying attitudes of mind, accepting or rejecting them on the basis of their knowledge of past art history and current trends.

Today many art students are dissuaded from copying the Old Masters, believing that they have no value for contemporary artists. The avant-garde galleries are thronged by young art students whenever famous pop painters are exhibiting. They return to their schools charged with the enthusiasm to emulate their idols. Such influences are not harmful as little in art is completely original. It was not long ago that art students crowded to see the works of Raphael. Now he has been demoted to a lower rank in the list of Old Master favourites. Until this century El Greco was not considered a particularly noteworthy artist. Today he is rated among the most popular painters.

Public taste and appreciation are capricious; works acceptable to one generation may be rejected by another, yet art of lasting quality will endure. The Old Masters' paintings have survived because they were painted with basically sound materials applied in a technique that ensured stability by craftsmen who learned their skills at an early age. Artists have profited from the accomplishments and mistakes of the preceding generations. The break from this tradition came when artists' colourmen placed oil pigments in transportable tube containers. This new mobility brought painting out-of-doors and created a revolution in the art world. Formerly paintings were contrived within the confines of the studio. Now painters were free to work on location. New styles and concepts of painting were evolved. The criteria established by past masters were swept aside. The doors were opened for experimentation and improvisation with methods and materials, which has led to a succession of problems for the restorer.

In the last few years artists have been going through a phase in which only the message is considered of importance and any means might be used to convey it. Unorthodox and impermanent materials seem both fashionable and desirable. Some contemporary art being produced will not survive for future generations to ponder. The artists have unwittingly built in their own means of destruction by the use of poor materials and unsound techniques. They may well be beyond the scope of future restoration.

OIL PAINTING

Oil paintings are created by using pigments suspended in oil, or an oil-based medium with varnish or turpentine. Several types of supports have been used for oil paints but canvas and panel remain the most popular and dependable.

The actual date of discovery of oil as a painting medium is a point that has been debated by art historians for generations. The identity of the first artist to use oil paints is open to conjecture, although many historians agree its development may be traced to the great Flemish artists Hubert and Jan Van Eyck in the early fifteenth century.

There are two basic techniques in oil painting. The first, a traditional method, requires the composition to be methodically constructed initially by underpainting. Colour layers and transparent glazes are painted over the underpainting to achieve the desired finish. In the second, a modern method, paint is applied directly (alla prima) to the primed support without underpainting. Painting is often carried out in a single day without necessitating drying time between applications. The final paint effect is sought from the initial brush stroke. The paint may be applied in broken tones of colour pigment with areas of ground exposed in thin washes, thick impasto layers or in any conceivable manner.

Traditional oil painting sometimes commenced with an underpainting in grey called *grisaille*. The neutral tone of grisaille could be either a warm or a cool grey over which colours were applied to complete the picture.

Examples of this method survive in unfinished works of the past and in a few instances when the artist obviously considered the grisaille painting a complete picture in itself.

Painters often worked on light or dark ground employing underpainting of umbers, greens or reds to establish the framework of the composition. The underpainting aided in placing areas of dark shadows, middle tones and light values. As time elapses, underpainting may begin to influence the overpainted layers of colour subtly, eventually affecting the tonality of the painting. Oil paints may be applied one over the other to achieve a rich effect. Glazes are made by painting a thin transparent dark colour over a lighter one.

The appearance and viscosity of the paint is of primary importance to the artist and may be described with the following terminology. *Short* paint refers to colour taken directly from the tube in a commercially prepared semi-gloss state. *Long* paint contains an oil medium making it easy to apply in long unbroken lines. The addition of an oil medium tends to make the colour appear *fat* or smooth and glossy. The paint must be thinned in order to make a *lean* paint which has a granular and matt appearance. To ensure stability, the natural order of building up a painting requires layers of lean paint to be applied before fat layers.

Oil paints remain the principal painting medium because of the many and varied ways they can be used. Perhaps their outstanding characteristic is that the paints can be re-worked and corrected when desired. They combine durability and colour tinting strength with ease of application and intermixing. They adhere to a great variety of supports and they are reasonably flexible. Above all, oil colours are most pleasing to the eye when properly used and they change little upon drying.

Oil paints have not been replaced for artists who desire control in the manipulation of their paints and a rich, full-bodied luminosity in the finished picture.

EGG TEMPERA

Egg tempera painting preceded oil painting by more than two centuries. It was used for most easel painting during the medieval and Renaissance periods. Sometimes it was employed in conjunction with oil paints or for underpainting.

Recipes for egg tempera abound, but the yolk of egg and water provide the purest unadulterated medium. Egg tempera has the unique characteristic of seeming to improve with time; as the colours harden, they become deeper and more transparent. Some recipes recommend the addition of an oil to the egg to facilitate fluid painting. This retards drying and the oil turns yellow, causing darkening and discolouration. Sometimes a preservative is added to keep the medium from spoiling. Any other adulterations are apt to cause future deterioration in the paint film.

Traditionally the most effective support for displaying the brilliant luminosity of tempera colours is a prepared gesso panel. Cennino Cennini gives the standard account of early panel preparations for egg tempera painting in his celebrated fifteenth-century treatise *Il Libro dell' Arte*. Egg tempera has a natural tenacity which enables it to adhere to most supports. The technique of tempera painting generally requires short individual strokes with small, pointed brushes, sometimes in a cross-hatching technique. The paint is built up gradually and dries rapidly to a hard, durable film. It is resistant to the effects of atmosphere and changes of temperature which, over a long period of time, might cause oil paints to crack.

If the medium and colours are mixed in the correct proportions they will bond in a texture neither too dry nor too glossy. The painting will have a soft, lustrous finish resembling that of an egg shell. If it has a dull appearance, it may be polished with a soft cloth or a varnish may be applied.

Modern manufacturing techniques have enabled egg tempera colours to be supplied in tubes for convenient use, although it is unlikely that anyone who has prepared his own egg tempera will find them entirely viable.

WATERCOLOUR

The watercolour technique is based on quick-drying transparent painting effects. An artist can obtain these by using applications of water and finely ground pigments suspended in an aqueous solution of gum arabic on a surface such as paper. Watercolour pigments have been known since ancient times. The preferred paper is handmade from linen rags. The paper is often allowed to show through and to provide a bright reflective base for the transparent colours painted over it.

Because watercolours on paper are susceptible to mould, dirt and stains, they must be protected under glass or in a drawer or folio. Watercolours kept in a suitable environment have remained stable over long periods of time. Gum or size used to bind the pigments are inclined to attract moisture, which can result in mould forming on the surface.

Exposure to strong light or dampness may affect fugitive colours. For example, indigo, a colour much favoured by early painters, oxidizes and turns brown upon prolonged exposure to air and light, as do most of the other natural dyestuffs. Prussian blue changes colour; chrome yellow turns a greenish hue and darkens; white lead, sometimes used as a body colour, is apt to blacken by absorbing sulphur from the air, which turns it into lead sulphide.

Watercolour painting remains one of the most direct means of expression. With quick decisive strokes, the artist may in a few minutes complete a picture that would require much longer with other media. Watercolour painting requires a discipline in its application as it cannot be removed or overpainted in an opaque manner without muddying the colours.

ENCAUSTIC

Encaustic paintings are made from pigments suspended in hot wax. It is one of the world's oldest sophisticated forms of painting. The Egyptians used encaustic paint on walls and on the outer panels of sarcophagi, representing the deceased with particular effectiveness. Exact descriptions of their technique have not been discovered. There is no evidence that it originated in Egypt nor are there any surviving classical Greek examples, although it was described in detail by Pliny.

One method of painting utilized wax into which pigments were introduced. The encaustic medium was then heated over a fire and applied in a liquid state with brush or knife. Another method required a hot iron which was passed over the previously laid pigment containing wax in a melting and fusing operation.

Paintings made with the wax medium have lasted astonishingly well without perceptibly yellowing as do pigments suspended in the oil medium. The waxes have remained stable and are impervious to water. The lasting advantages would seem to favour encaustic painting over almost any other media, were it not for the difficulty that its application can hamper the artist's technique and thus his vision.

Modern encaustic colours are obtainable in tubes, but when compared with the fine Egyptian Fayum district portraits, the results are unfavourable. Contemporary painters, such as Diego Rivera, have revived the encaustic painting method using heat lamps and electric spatulas to fuse the wax and pigment.

FRESCO

The Italians have contributed the names for many of the processes in both painting and restoring frescoes. There are two major techniques of fresco painting: *buon* fresco and fresco *secco*. Buon fresco is painting on a wall still damp with fresh plaster. Fresco secco is painting on a plastered wall that has dried and hardened.

The underlying plaster is composed of lime mortar mixed with marble, sand or grit, while the final layers contain only lime mortar. The colours that are mixed with water and painted directly on to the plaster must be resistant to the lime mixture by which they are absorbed and bound.

Guide drawings were made on walls in preparation for painting frescoes. They were referred to as *sinopia* because of the red earth pigments used to outline the general composition on to the *arriccio*, a first rough plaster. The rough layer incorporating the sinopia red drawing was covered with a layer of smoother plaster called the *intonaco*. This smooth layer was applied wet over the rough plaster in an area that the artist could cover in one day's painting before it dried. The sinopia disappeared under the plaster but was rapidly retraced over the new smooth plaster layer. The painting progressed day by day with freshly applied plaster joining the edges of the previous day's work.

Sinopia drawings have been revealed by the *stacco* method of detaching the painting when the plaster has begun to deteriorate. This modern restoring process removes both the paint and the intonaco layer, revealing the sinopia drawing in the rough arriccio plaster. Both may be preserved for viewing as individual works. To detach a painting with the stacco method, an animal glue is applied over the paint surface and separate layers of calico and canvas are adhered. When they have dried, they are pulled from the wall, taking the plaster and painting with them. The excess plaster is scraped from the back and a new cloth is attached. The facing cloths are removed and the fresco is ready for transfer to a new support.

Another method of transferring composition guide lines to the final plaster layer employed a full-scale drawing on paper known as a cartoon. The cartoon was pricked with holes at intervals along the drawn lines. Dusting or pouncing chalk placed in a cloth bag was tapped along the lines to penetrate the holes and appear on the plaster as an outline of the drawing.

Synthetic Painting Media

The introduction of synthetic materials for painting has changed the concepts and techniques of many artists using traditional media. Synthetic materials offer a new freedom of expression suited to the development of new art forms. Traditionally, only pigments have been bound in the various media. Now sand, gravel, wood and many other substances may be used and adhered to a support by synthetic binders. Unlike most traditional media, these paints adhere to a variety of surfaces and can be readily applied in thick layers.

The rapid drying properties of synthetic paints are at the same time advantageous and disconcerting. These paints may be built quickly, layer upon layer, without lengthy drying time between each additional layer. Oil paints used in this manner would certainly crack. On the other hand, the artist does not always want his colours to dry rapidly and become unworkable.

Synthetic paints are ideally suited for field trips or for excursions abroad. Their versatility and adaptability to supports make them particularly desirable for locations where art supplies are limited or non-existent. It should be noted that hot climatic conditions increase the paint's drying rate on the palette and they are not resoluble.

In classrooms, particularly those of lower age levels, synthetic paints provide a new exciting adventure. Paints that are on a professional level with oils, easily manipulated and readily removed from clothes, hands and furniture, are a boon to the art teacher. In addition, they are non-toxic and non-inflammable, and they adhere to a wide variety of inexpensive supports.

Artists who suffer from allergies such as skin or eye irritations which are aggravated by the substances in oils have found the use of synthetic paints a means of continuing their work.

Manufacturers claim that the qualities of synthetic paints surpass those of traditional media and have none of their deficiencies. They have a high degree of clarity which remains stable for the lifetime of the material, and they are non-yellowing, non-cracking and quick drying. They would seem to be the ideal media but it will be many years before the test of time can prove their prophecies.

A number of restoration laboratories are conducting tests to study the behaviour of the new synthetic materials under specific conditions. The materials are tested to determine the degree of shrinkage, cracking during stress, weathering and fading of colours and resistance to solvents. Restorers are most anxious to ascertain the problems they may be required to rectify in the future. Indeed, problems of stability are already becoming evident with some contemporary synthetic media pictures.

The increasing number of artists questioning the permanency of synthetic painting materials is an indication of their concern about the craft of painting and the longevity of their work. It is hoped this respect for painting materials will lead to a closer relationship between the artist and the restorer.

THE PREPARATION OF POLYMER TEMPERA

There are two distinct media available under the broad term 'polymer tempera'. One is made from polyvinyl acetate while the other is formulated with acrylic resin. Both are made from emulsions.

Briefly, polymer emulsion is composed of solid particles of synthetic resins dispersed in water. The water is allowed to evaporate and the resin crystals unite to form a white continuous film.

Paint manufacturers buy the polymer emulsion from specialist firms and prepare it by adding pigments, dispersants, wetting agents and anti-foaming agents. Thickeners are added to increase the viscosity and to give the polymer tempera a consistency comparable to oil paints. Retarders are put into the paint to prevent it from drying too rapidly. Finally, preservatives must be included to prevent mould or mildew growth.

The colours are then put into jars, squeeze-type plastic bottles, or polythene tubes. The latter have been found to retain moisture longer than metal or polyvinyl cellulose tubes. The paint should remain in a pliable state for about three years.

POLYMER TEMPERA (ACRYLIC BASE)

Acrylic resins, polyvinyl acetate, the expoxies and polyesters are man-made inventions which have become most useful to the artist. Of all the synthetic products created in the chemist's laboratory since the invention of bakelite at the turn of the century, none has been more useful to the artist than acrylic resin.

Acrylic resins have been mixed with colour pigments to create new media. They differ greatly from the traditional painting media of the past. It would be very difficult, for instance, to make a deceptive forgery of an oil painting using acrylic paints.

Acrylic paints may be used in various techniques. They may be thinly diluted with water and used as watercolours on paper. The colours may be overlaid in washes, or with only slight dilution they take on a consistency desirable for tempera painting. By the addition of less water and more paint a gouache effect is obtained which is suitable for work on flexible paper or fashion board. They may be applied like oils as a full-bodied paint directly from the tube on to canvas or panel employing impasto brush work or painting knife techniques. They can also be used for collage with paper, string, or bits of stone and wood impressed into the paint. These will be bound in the paint upon drying. Paint rollers, sponges or spatter techniques may be used with equanimity. Although a water-based medium, the paint becomes impervious to water after drying.

Upon completion of the painting, the acrylic colours, which like tempera dry by the evaporation of water, appear to have more sheen than tempera but less than most oil colours. Final picture varnishes are made especially for the synthetic paints and it is recommended that no other varnish should be used.

Normally acrylics are miscible only in water. They do not mix satisfactorily with any other media such as oil paints, watercolour and tempera or with dilutents like turpentine or turpentine substitute. Such additives will reduce their elasticity and cause future problems.

A solution polymer (acrylic base) which claims to be compatible with oil paints has been made available to artists.

POLYMER TEMPERA (POLYVINYL ACETATE BASE)

Polymer tempera paints formulated from polyvinyl acetate are vying with acrylics for popularity amongst artists. Alfred Duca is given credit for having developed the first polymer tempera medium from experiments begun in 1945 in the USA. Polymer tempera medium is a highly polymerized grade of polyvinyl acetate.

Practically all of the merits and techniques described for acrylic polymer tempera are applicable to the polyvinyl acetate medium. They may be applied in watercolour washes and thin glazes or directly from the tube in thick layers.

I have worked with acrylics and PVA paints and have found little difference in handling behaviour between the two, although polyvinyl acetate provides somewhat stronger adhesion and a harder film, giving it some protective advantages.

The compatability of the various brands of polymer tempera on the market is somewhat dubious due to various manufacturer's additives. Therefore, it is inadvisable for the artist to mix the various brands.

The two synthetic media discussed are not the only ones being manufactured for artists but they are by far the most commercially successful. A natural painting medium, casine tempera, popular for many years in America, has similarities comparable to the synthetic paints. Traditional casine is composed of white curd from skim milk combined with slaked lime and then emulsified. The pigments prepared by contemporary manufacturers have additives and are miscible with water.

Several years ago I painted a number of pictures with casine tempera, using them to imitate watercolour, tempera, gouache and oil paints quite convincingly. Some of the colours began to harden in the tubes rather quickly but this tendency has no doubt been rectified.

Pigments

A complete list of pigments and their properties would require a text filling two large volumes. New colours and names are constantly being introduced by manufacturers. Although under the guise of new pigments, many are merely tints of existing colours.

A restorer with knowledge of the composition of pigments, the periods when they were in use and their application by various artists and schools of painting, has an invaluable asset in his profession.

Almost every book published on the materials and techniques of artists contains a chapter devoted to the various characteristics of colour pigments. In view of the abundance of material available in print about modern colours manufactured for the contemporary artist, it would seem more relevant in this book to review a few of the pigments from natural sources which were used in the past. Many are colours the restorer may encounter in cleaning, others have an historical interest. Some of them are still important today while others have disappeared or have been replaced by superior artificially made colours. This list is fragmentary and contains little regarding the technical and chemical composition of manufacture. It is meant simply to introduce these colours to readers in the hope that it will act as a stimulus to seek additional information from more specialized sources.

Pigments from Natural Resources

The pigments in this list are either *organic* or *inorganic*. The organic pigments are composed of carbon and other elements and include madders, carmine, crimson lake, gamboge, indigo and various colours derived from coal or tar.

The inorganic colours include those derived from the combination of various substances with metals to form oxides and sulphides such as red and yellow ochre, genuine ultramarine blue, terre verte and vermilion.

AZURITE (*mountain blue*)

Azurite is an azure blue vitreous mineral of basic copper carbonate. It was usually coarsely ground for painting because of limited tinting power when finely ground. Azurite has been known since antiquity and it was the principal blue pigment in European paintings for nearly two hundred years from the fifteenth century to the seventeenth century. It is often confused with lapis lazuli, which it resembles.

BITUMEN (*asphaltum*)

Bitumen is a brownish-black mineral pitch found in oil-producing regions. It was generally used by the Old Masters in resinous reddish-brown glazes, which have survived relatively well. Eighteenth-century British painters delighted in using bitumen liberally, much to the detriment of their paint films, which have shrunk and cracked in irregular patterns. Bitumen is highly discredited as a pigment and it is not used today for oil painting.

BLACK

IVORY BLACK is the richest and deepest black. It is made by charring animal bones. Ivory black has a transparency and permanency suitable for glazing with oil.

LAMP BLACK, CARBON and CHARCOAL BLACK are hydrocarbons of a tar made from the soot generated by the partial burning or carbonizing of gas, wood or oil. They are some of the cheapest and easiest pigments for the artist to make himself.

VINE BLACK and PEACH BLACK are of vegetable origin, made from the calcination of vine twigs and peach or apricot pits. They tend to have a rather bluish tone.

BLUE VERDITER (*blue bice*)

Blue verditer was often employed as a substitute for the more costly and throughout the eighteenth century, although it lacked permanence. Blue verditer was often employed as a substitute for the more costly ultramarine and azurite pigments.

COCHINEAL (*carmine and crimson lake*) AND OTHER NATURAL DYESTUFFS

COCHINEAL is made from the dried insect coccus cacti, which thrives on cactus from Mexico to South America. Cochineal is a natural dyestuff. It is purported to have been introduced into European painting by returning Spanish traders following the conquest of Mexico.

INDIGO is a blue dye obtained from indigo or related plants grown in many parts of the world but principally in India. It has been known since antiquity. Indigo was used as a tempera paint in medieval times and as an oil colour into the eighteenth century. It is now produced synthetically.

KERMES or Kermes lake is another of the natural dyestuffs derived from insect bodies found in the Mediterranean region. It was replaced as a pigment in the Middle Ages by *lac* or Indian lake. The latter was obtained from an insect secretion.

MADDER or madder lake came from a root cultivated in classical times in both Europe and Asia Minor. It has largely been replaced by Alizarin.

SAP GREEN was obtained from the ripened berries of buckthorn. Although it is a fugitive colour, it was used on illuminated manuscripts where it has survived relatively well. Modern oil paints bearing the name sap green are usually made from coal tar lakes.

GREEN EARTH (*terre verte*)

Most green earths probably originated as marine clays composed of magnesium, hydrous iron and aluminium potassium silicates. Deposits of green earth are found near Verona, Italy, and also in Germany and France. It was used extensively by the Italian Renaissance painters to underpaint and model flesh tones. With the passing of time, green earth has had a decided darkening influence on the colours overlying it.

INDIAN YELLOW

The original source of Indian yellow pigment was the urine of Indian cattle fed on pureed mango leaves. Through a series of washing and drying, the pigment becomes a golden yellow. It is now prepared synthetically from coal tars.

IRON OXIDE RED

Iron oxides are obtained from natural sources the world over. They are of hydrous and anhydrous ferric oxide varying in hue from yellow to maroon. They have been used since the prehistoric cave painters and can be considered absolutely permanent. Some varieties of the important iron oxide pigments are haematite, Indian and light red, Mars colours, Tuscan and Venetian red.

The earth colours require grinding, sieving, washing and levigation to prepare them for fine colour pigments. They are usually classed as permanent colours.

MALACHITE

Malachite is a deep green mineral carbonate of copper often carved for ornamental stoneware. It was prepared as a pigment by grinding and sieving. It was employed as an important green pigment from ancient times and by Flemish and Italian artists from the fourteenth to sixteenth centuries.

MASSICOT (litharge)

A yellow oxide of lead prepared by roasting metallic or white lead is called massicot. It has been identified in a number of Dutch and Flemish paintings executed between the fifteenth and seventeenth centuries.

MINIUM (orange lead)

Another pigment produced by subjecting white lead to roasting was minium. The colour varied according to the amount of heat and the duration of the roasting. It has been sometimes confused with red lead, which is still used for anti-corrosive purposes on iron and steel.

NAPLES YELLOW (antimony yellow)

The heating together of lead and antimony oxides produces Naples yellow. Genuine Naples yellow is semi-transparent. It was used in ancient times for ceramic glazes and by the early oil painters. Although still manufactured, it is gradually disappearing from the artist's palette as it is prone to darkening.

OCHRE (brown, golden, red and yellow ochre)

Ochres are native earths coloured by iron oxide. They are found in many parts of the world. Yellow ochre was used in ancient Egypt and has been an important colour in all the periods of European painting history.

Red ochre was referred to in ancient and medieval times as sinopia, after Sinope, a town in Asia Minor where the choicest red earth was found.

Ochres are ground and washed free of iron sulphate compounds in their preparation. They are all permanent colours and vary considerably in tone depending upon their manufacture.

ORPIMENT

Orpiment is a brilliant lemon-yellow sulphide of arsenic used as a pigment from classical times to the end of the eighteenth century. It is little used today due to its highly poisonous content. Orpiment is generally found well preserved in illuminated manuscripts. Early manuscripts kept in a protected state permitted many fugitive colours to retain much of their original brilliance, whereas the same pigments used for paintings have discoloured.

REALGAR

Realgar is a soft orange-red arsenic ore usually found in close relationship to orpiment in natural deposits. It is used today in tanning and pyrotechnics. Realgar resembles red lead and has been known since ancient times.

SIENNA (burnt and raw sienna)

Sienna is a special clay containing iron and manganese oxides. Sienna derives its name from the Italian city where the best grades are still found. Burnt sienna is prepared by calcining raw sienna. Because of its transparency, raw sienna has been used frequently for glazing. Both colours are considered permanent.

SMALT

Finely powdered cobalt glass was used to make the lovely blue colour of smalt. It was used largely by seventeenth-century painters although it has been known since antiquity. Smalt has been identified in a few paintings by Rubens.

ULTRAMARINE BLUE, NATURAL (lapis lazuli)

Lapis lazuli is an opaque azure-blue gemstone of the mineral lazurite found in many parts of the world. The best quality is found in remote areas of Afghanistan.

Natural ultramarine was expensive and highly prized as a colour by artists and as a gemstone by lapidaries. It has been used from medieval times principally for brilliant blue robes and garments. It was used to a lesser extent than azurite, which was less costly and more easily obtainable. It gradually disappeared after 1800 when experiments with the manufacture of artificial ultramarine blue proved successful.

Although almost non-existent in the past few years, natural ultramarine has been revived recently by Winsor & Newton Limited of Harrow, Middlesex. They have obtained a supply of fine quality lapis lazuli with which they have been able to manufacture a limited amount of genuine ultramarine blue pigment in the traditional method advised by Cennino Cennini. There will probably not be a stampede by art students to purchase this rare pigment as the price works out to roughly twice its equivalent weight in gold.

UMBER (*raw and burnt umber*)

Raw umber is a reddish-brown earth composed of ferric oxide, silica, alumina and manganese oxides. Some of the best quality deposits are found in Cyprus.

Burnt umber is produced by roasting the raw umber earth until the proper shade of colour is attained. The umbers were not generally used in European painting until after the fifteenth century.

VAN DYKE BROWN (*Cassel and Cologne earth*)

Most of the brown earth used to produce Van Dyke brown comes from Germany in the Cassel and Cologne areas. It has been used in the past for shadows, backgrounds and glazing. Because of the manganese content, some of these pigments are fugitive when exposed to light.

VERDIGRIS

The pigment verdigris is a poisonous blue or green basic copper acetate made by the action of acetic acid on copper. Verdigris has been known since antiquity and extensively used in the illumination of medieval books and manuscripts. It was used by the Van Eycks and their followers and by the Venetian painters principally for glazing. Verdigris continued in popular use into the sixteenth century. It has been replaced by viridian.

WHITE LEAD

The extensively used white-lead pigment has been given many names: it is called flake white, cremnitz white or blanc d'argent. It is a basic lead carbonate made by a process which begins with the exposure of lead sheets to acetic acid vapours. They undergo a complex series of reactions and are finally converted into highly poisonous white lead.

Pliny described it as the most important lead pigment known in ancient times. White lead was used in Egyptian encaustic paintings and in most pictures of importance until the nineteenth century.

Artists' Palettes

The choice of colour pigments for an artist's palette is highly individual. Countless recommendations have been offered as to the ideal range of pigments that he should select. Artists seldom have identical colour palettes but several important permanent pigments appear with regularity over many generations.

The following lists of artists' pigments used by two outstanding colourists separated by more than a century may be compared:

THE PALETTE OF PETER PAUL RUBENS (1577-1640)

Burnt sienna	Ultramarine blue (genuine)
Ivory black	Vermilion
Madder	Vert azure (oxide of cobalt)
Malachite	White lead
Orpiment	Yellow lake
Red ochre	Yellow ochre

THE PALETTE OF J. M. W. TURNER (1776-1851)

The paint box displayed at the Tate Gallery, London, is indicative of the pigments in use by nineteenth century British artists. Turner obtained combinations of hues with these pigments that few artists could emulate. They were analysed by Dr. J. S. Gourlay as follows:

Gamboge	Purple oxide
Prussian blue	Raw sienna
Indian red	Carbon black
Yellow ochre	Bone black
Chrome yellow	Terre verte
Native chalk	Vermilion
Cobalt blue	Venetian red
Orange lead	Blue verditer (basic copper carbonate)
Barium yellow	Turner's yellow (basic lead chloride—
Midchrome yellow	probably safflower on alumina
Mercuric iodine	base)
Orange chrome	Madder lake

'St Anthony Abbot' (detail). Ascribed to Bartolo di Fredi (1353-1410). Reproduced by courtesy of the Trustees, the National Gallery, London. A gilded panel with holes made by worms (now inactive). Punch marks and incised lines decorate the halo

Gold Leaf Preparation

The modern process of gold beating provides gold leaf mainly for gilding frames and furniture although a few artists and heraldic illustrators still use it in their work. The gold is melted and cast into a bar. It is then passed through rollers until it is flattened into a ribbon 1/1000th-inch thick from which 200 two-inch squares are cut and placed between pieces of vellum to form a *cutch*, which is encased in parchment to withstand the first beating.

The process requires four separate stages of beating, which is done in a rhythmic pattern with heavy hammers. The gold leaf is flattened outwards to extend beyond its original dimensions. After each beating, the enlarged leaves are removed and divided into quarters by means of a cane knife with two parallel blades called a *waggon*. During the third and fourth beatings, the sheets are interleaved with *goldbeater's skin*, a membrane made from the intestines of an ox. The final beating, which takes three and one-half hours, is in a *mould*. Sixty-four of the one-inch gold squares in the mould have come from each two-inch square originally cut from the ribbon.

The leaves are finally cut into three and one quarter-inch squares and laid on to rouged tissue with wooden pincers and puffs of breath. The sheets of tissue are in a book holding twenty-five gold leaves when filled. The leaves are so thin (1/250,000th of an inch) that, when held up, light is visible through them.

Gilding

Gilding is the art of applying gold leaf or gold dust to any suitable material. Gold leaf was used extensively in panel paintings of the Byzantine period. As time passed it was used to a lesser extent, mostly on painted ornaments or haloes, until it finally became an embellishment for expensive frames and furniture.

Panel paintings carried the gold leaf embedded in the smooth gesso ground where it was often burnished and tooled. Punches of various designs were used to form decorative patterns in the leaf.

The lavish use of gold leaf in medieval pictures was in part due to the dark interiors of the churches. The pictures were often hung in gloomy recesses and illuminated by candlelight so that the gold reflected the light with a flickering brilliance.

The leaf, although extremely thin, will outlast paint. Gold leaf is used on statues permanently displayed out-of-doors and on the exterior of cathedral domes and decorative plaques. For example, the gold leaf used on the Queen Victoria Memorial in front of Buckingham Palace need only be renewed every hundred years.

OIL GILDING AND WATER GILDING

The two methods commonly used to lay gold leaf are oil gilding and water gilding. Oil gilding may be employed when it is intended that the leaf remain unburnished in a natural matt finish. The methods of preparation are similar to those used in water gilding with the exception that an oil gold size replaces the water.

Preparing a surface for water gilding, whether it be a wooden panel or a frame, requires a suitably laid gesso ground. The gesso is applied in several even coats with drying time allowed in between. It is then finely sanded and wiped with a cloth.

A *bole* (coloured earth clay) is mixed with parchment or gelatine size to the consistency of thin cream. The bole may be red or yellow to give a warm tone to the gold leaf laid over it. Blue or black bole may be used to provide a cool tone. A mop brush is dipped into the bole/size mixture and lightly brushed over the gesso. Four or five coats of bole are usually sufficient for bright burnishing of the gold. The bole surface is prepared for gilding by sanding and polishing.

The gold leaf is laid on to a leather cushion aided by gentle puffs of breath. The leaf is cut with a special gilding knife to the required size. It is then collected on a wide flat brush of fine animal hair called a *tip*. The bole surface is lightly brushed with water and the gold is carefully laid so that it barely overlaps adjoining pieces. Small pockets of trapped air that appear under the gold are flattened by gentle tapping with a soft brush. The panel is left to dry upon completion of laying the gold. It should be burnished before the underlying bole has dried hard.

Burnishing is the process by which the gold is given a brilliant appearance. The instrument used for burnishing is a specially polished stone, usually an agate, mounted on a handle. The burnisher is drawn across the easily scratched gold in long even strokes, using light hand pressure.

There is at present a resurgence of gilding and the use of gold leaf in modern paintings, prints and sculpture. In addition to the traditional gold, other metals such as silver and platinum leaf are becoming popular.

CHAPTER VI

PAINTING EXAMINATION

A great many paintings examined will have been restored at one time or another. Some of these may be perfectly sound. Others may have been seriously damaged through over-zealous cleaning, lining with unsuitable glue, darkening of oil paint retouches, or any number of inappropriate practices. In fact, one of the restorer's most frequent tasks is the minimizing or removal of previous restorations.

In order to establish a case history for restoration, a painting must be thoroughly examined. The essential categories of examination may be divided into three groups: visual, photographic, and analytic with scientific apparatus. Some scientific tests are both costly and time-consuming. A painting should be examined in depth only in so far as its historical importance and possible preservation warrant. A visual examination costs nothing. The restorer's ability to recognize the causes of deterioration is based on his knowledge and experience. There are many similarities between a doctor examining a patient and the restorer examining a painting. If the diagnosis reveals a minor ailment, treatment may commence. If the problem is more complex, scientific aids must be employed and further investigation by specialists proposed.

Some apparatuses are not generally available in small restoration studios and laboratories. The examination is described in this book, whenever possible, in the normal procedural sequence. This may vary according to individual preferences, priorities or the type of equipment at hand.

There are many investigatory aids available to the restorer. Restoration centres which specialize in scientific developments use more complex paraphernalia for detailed examination than the limited equipment of the private restorer may permit. Some of the larger art museums employ a scientific research staff who conduct experiments and test new inventions and materials for their efficiency and stability. Modern industrial technology continually provides new ideas and materials which are of value to art restoration.

Part I. Visual

An understanding of the anatomy of a painting, the materials and methods used by artists and the causes of deterioration together with the ability to recognize former restorations or overpainting are essential for effective examination of pictures and their ultimate preservation. Some artists used techniques and materials that were later proven unstable. Other artists applied tints and glazes which, if unrecognized, might be lost in the process of cleaning. The restorer, in carrying out his examination, must be constantly aware of the pitfalls that might lie ahead in the consolidation and cleaning of the painting.

The initial examination of a painting may be carried out with the naked eye in good light. Observations made at this time are noted for further investigation with the scientific equipment available to the restorer. Few restorers are fortunate to have in their studios a vast range of equipment. Certain investigations, such as X-ray and pigment analysis, may require the use of laboratories with more specialized knowledge and facilities.

Modern techniques of examination can reveal layer by layer the composition of a painting through the varnish, paint, ground and support. Long-buried mysteries have been solved, fascinating discoveries have been made and the artist's intentions and methods more fully understood. These techniques guide the restorer and historian in carrying out their work.

A complete written record of the first examination of a painting is kept. Each condition and its probable cause are noted. Thereafter, written and photographic documentation of the step-by-step analysis and treatment will establish a permanent dossier for future examinations of the painting.

The principal conditions and their causes which may adversely affect a painting are described in this chapter. The procedures for treatment of these conditions are presented in the ensuing chapters on Consolidation, Cleaning, Retouching and Revarnishing.

The Varnish Layer

The protective layer of varnish may have undergone many chemical changes. Varnished pictures may be affected by extremes of darkness and damp or conversely by over-exposure to sunlight and heat. Scratches and accidents of all kinds may have pitted the surface. Dust and dirt will accumulate in these crevices unless the old varnish is removed and a new varnish applied.

Most varnishes encountered in examination will be of either oil or resin composition. Eighteenth- and nineteenth-century paintings were frequently varnished with a natural resin such as dammar or mastic.

A fair idea of the picture underlying the old varnish layers can be obtained by passing a small wad of clean, fine cotton wool dipped in white spirit lightly over the surface. In the United States the nearest equivalent of white spirit is called mineral spirit. The best grade cotton wool should always be used and then discarded. White spirit is mild and highly volatile, so that no harm can occur unless the area is kept continually soaked. Evaporation takes place within seconds. This is extremely important as any cracks in the varnish, many so fine they are not visible, will absorb water or solvents causing damage to the paint surface and the ground.

UNVARNISHED PAINTINGS

Not all paintings have been varnished. Paintings were frequently sold from artists' studios before a final picture varnish had been applied. Most of these have been subsequently varnished although some have survived in an unvarnished state.

The process of removing dirt from an unvarnished painting is potentially as hazardous as removing varnish. Extreme care must be exercised during this procedure as there is no protective film between the cleaning agent and the paint.

Paintings in tempera pigments were often left unvarnished because the egg yolk painting medium gave them a natural lustre or sheen. The high gloss that varnish imparts was not always considered desirable for tempera colours.

DISCOLOURED VARNISH

The most obvious indication that a picture requires cleaning is the disintegration of the varnish. Protective layers of varnish darken and obscure the underlying paint colours with their yellow-brown film. The ravages of time and environmental conditions reduce the varnish's longevity and ultimately that of the paint if the embrittled varnish is not removed. Mellow colours of old paintings are usually an optical illusion created by discoloured varnish. Underneath lie the true colours waiting to be revealed.

Small cleaning tests are usually carried out to determine the resistance of the varnish, retouches and original paint to certain solvents. The test areas are normally not much larger than a postage stamp and located at the edges of the composition or in relatively insignificant passages.

BLOOM

A cloudy bluish-white discolouration appearing in the picture varnish layer is called *bloom*. This condition is generally considered to be the result of moisture penetration of natural resin varnishes, although other opinions exist as to the cause of its formation. Pictures exposed to a damp atmosphere appear the most vulnerable. Another factor which may contribute to the bloom condition suggests that unsuitable materials were used in the varnish composition. Modern synthetic varnishes are much less likely to bloom than the natural varnishes.

BLANCHING

Similar in appearance to bloom, but with a more greyish opaqueness, *blanching* often occurs after the removal of old varnish. Many restorers consider this to be caused by the inability of the particular solvent used to dissolve the varnish layer completely. The varnish residue remaining on the paint layer quickly blanches. Certain solvents, apparently those containing a high proportion of water, would seem to be at fault.

CRAZING AND CRAQUELURE

The minute network of small cracks appearing in varnish but not yet penetrating through the layers of paint is called *crazing*. It is generally due to improperly prepared varnish mixtures that have lost their bond. The cracks may eventually deepen to affect the paint beneath.

The word *craquelure* is used to describe the familiar cracking observed in older paintings that has penetrated the varnish and paint layers. They are sometimes referred to as age cracks.

The Paint Layer

A painting's continued survival often depends upon the artist's selection of materials and his technique in applying them. Mistakes in the construction of a painting may limit the extent of future restorations; for example, fugitive colours cannot be revived. The excessive use of oils and dryers in the pigments may cause deep cracks and wrinkles which are difficult to rectify. The deleterious effects of bitumen employed as a pigment cannot be eradicated. Paint applied to a canvas in thin turpentine washes (a technique favoured by the impressionists) proffers a problem for the future. The opposite extreme, paint applied in unusually thick layers with insufficient drying time allowed between coats, will ultimately cause disfiguration.

CRACKS

The ageing process of a painting affects its structure. Some develop *cracks* more quickly than others depending upon the soundness of construction and the judicious choice of material. Cracks can appear in the varnish layer without actually penetrating through to the paint. If the paint has not been affected, restoration is made easier as the cracks will disappear with the removal of the varnish. Old paintings lose elasticity in the paint layers and ground. Cracking in these layers is generally the result of tensions at work within the structure. The effects of ageing and drying produce a craquelure, or fine network cracking, in practically all old paintings. Prolonged movement, instability of the support or inadvertent pressures cause disfiguration if left unattended. Changes of temperature and environment can cause the support to expand and contract producing cracks that penetrate through the ground to the paint and varnish layers. Allowed to continue, the stress of movement produces a widening of the cracks and further splitting.

Spiral cracks appear frequently in lean chalk grounds and paints on thin canvas. They are often caused by a knock at the back or the improper lifting of a picture by grasping the stretcher support from behind with the fingers, thereby putting pressure against the canvas sufficient to cause concentric cracking. Fishbone cracks, as the name indicates, resemble a fish's spine. They derive from abnormal stress such as the tight rolling of a painting. Poorly keyed stretchers can cause stress in the support effecting cracks in the paint structure.

A form of dry cracking or traction cracking is caused by a final varnish having been painted over partially dried oil paint. The condition increases as the films slowly dry. Traction cracking is irregular in appearance, rather resembling frosted tree branches. This is due to pronounced cracking in overlying dark colours which exposes light paint or ground beneath. Cracking seldom occurs in white pigments or paint mixed with white unless they are applied too thickly.

Another type of cracking is produced by the excessive use of bitumen. In the nineteenth century artists were ecstatic over the golden glow imparted by the transparent bitumen pigment. Its use was especially prevalent

An example of spiral cracking

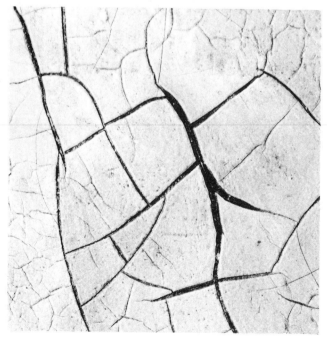

Cracks resulting from the separation of the paint layers over unseasoned ground

Bitumen cracking in a nineteenth-century painting

in British paintings. The presence of bitumen colour is usually recognizable by the extensive separation of the paint or by a rough texture resembling alligator skin. This soft treacly colour, if used liberally, seldom dries completely and, as with road tar, the presence of heat can make it melt, bubble and flow. Paint separates into islands surrounded by wide channels of exposed ground. The greatly deteriorated paintings of the American romantic painter Albert Pinkham Ryder are examples of the consequences of large quantities of bitumen. Evidence exists that bitumen was used much earlier than the nineteenth century but it was mainly applied in thin glazes which did not create problems. Fortunately for artists and restorers alike, the damaging effects of bitumen were realized and its use was discontinued.

Cracks in modern paintings are often the consequence of using inferior materials. Overly absorbent supports or primings will suck the binding media from the paint, accelerating unnatural drying, resulting in cracks. The addition of excessive dryers and extenders or foreign elements, such as sand introduced to create a texture, is also responsible for cracking.

CLEAVAGE

A painting develops *cleavage* when the support contracts resulting in the loss of bond between the ground and support or laminated layers of the paint. Cleavage or buckling is not always visible in the early stages. The loss of adhesion may at first appear as a slightly inflated air pocket rising from the paint surface. As the contraction progresses, the cleavage may manifest itself by fracturing at the apex of the swelling and around the base. Occasionally cleavage may be caused by shrinking of the adhesive used in glue-lined canvases.

CUPPING

A curling or *cupping* of the paint may accompany the cleavage as a result of further stresses in the support. Intersecting cracks form small islands in the paint film and the loss of adhesion causes the paint edges to curl upwards. Water permeating a canvas support can weaken the binding power of the ground and cause the paint to swell and cup. In its most severe form, the cupped paint edges overlap each other.

FLAKING

The movement and stresses of the support are instrumental in cracking and cleavage of the layers, causing the paint to lose bond and become

Flaking paint under a raking light

Wrinkling due to excess oil in the paint

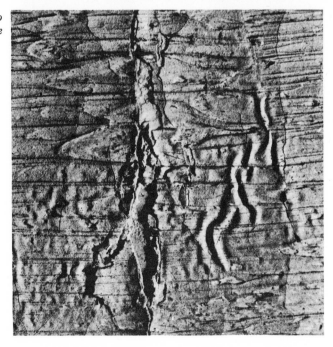

detached. This condition is called *flaking*. Prolonged exposure to excessive atmospheric humidity is frequently a factor in this breakdown of the painting structure. Areas of overpainting in a picture are particularly prone to flaking under these deleterious conditions. In addition to moisture absorbed from environmental atmosphere, the past practice of washing paintings with water is responsible for a great deal of structural damage. Flaking may occur in the varnish layer only without affecting the paint.

Cracking and flaking in some paintings, whether old or modern, have often been the fault of the artist's painting technique. The colours should be painted initially in lean layers, building towards fat. The reverse, commencing with fat layers and finishing with lean, is unsound.

WRINKLING

The excessive use of fatty oils such as linseed oil in the painting medium is in many instances responsible for *wrinkling* in the paint layer. Paintings containing bitumen sometimes exhibit wrinkling, as will paint applied in very thick layers with insufficient drying time between applications. These have a tendency to develop sliding in the wet and unstable lower paint strata. The effect on the surface paint film is the formation of wrinkles or heavy folds. Turning the picture upside down, thus allowing the direction of the slide to reverse itself, will halt the movement temporarily but it does not offer a remedy.

Paint squeezed on a palette and allowed to dry is an example of this process in action. The surface film dries on exposure to air while the protected paint beneath remains tacky for weeks. This outer skin forms wrinkles, contracts and shrivels. The artist may lift aside this skin with his palette knife and find the underlying paint nearly as fresh as when it was squeezed from the tube. A painting can have layers of underlying colour that stay soft for many years or in the case of bitumen the paint may remain in a state of suspension.

BLISTERING

Cleavage may appear in the form of a *blister* before stresses induce a fracture. More pronounced blistering will occur in paint exposed to extreme heat or actual fire. These blisters are considerably more fragile than those caused by humidity and detachment. The heat blister is thin and brittle and should not be touched with the fingers lest it disintegrate.

PENTIMENTI

The passage of time can affect the oil medium by causing a transparency

'Allegory: War and Peace' (detail) by *Jacob Jordaens* (1593–1678). *Detail in raking light. The blisters are caused by loss of adhesion in an earlier relining*

known as *pentimenti* to develop. Pentimenti is literally a bleeding through of underlying layers which allows the initial drawing or painting to become visible. This phenomenon made possible the only glimpses of the early painters' first tentative strokes and subsequent alterations until modern scientific aids permitted examination in depth. The pentimenti becomes so transparent in some paintings that drawn guidelines in graphite and charcoal on the priming layer are clearly visible.

A canvas re-used for painting over an earlier composition may be revealed in time by the colours becoming transparent. A classic example of pentimenti is the seventeenth-century painting by Pieter De Hooch, 'An Interior with a Woman Drinking with Two Men' in the collection of the National Gallery, London. The tessellated floor may be readily observed through the now transparent skirt of the maidservant.

Pentimenti in a painting cannot be altered, although an old varnish may serve to obscure it. In the past it has been overpainted, a practice no longer considered ethical. Many scholars and art historians prefer to see this visible evidence of the artist's technique exposed to view rather than hidden.

ABRASION
Pictures are subject to all kinds of *abrasions* from accidental knocks to neglect and overcleaning. Scratches occur most frequently when the picture is being transported. Art exhibition entry forms stress the removal of picture eyes and wire to prevent damage to other paintings. Geometric paintings of the hard-edge school are frequently disfigured in transit. A single scratch on a precisely gradated paint surface can be disastrous. Few of these paintings are protected by varnish, since the matt effect is considered most desirable. The retouching of abrasions must be carried out with considerable skill and the minimal application of paint. Overall colour harmony and unity of the painting must be borne in mind.

Previous Restorations

The examination of a picture involves not only establishing the nature of the processes at work in the deterioration of the structure but also the detection of previous restorations. A trained restorer can soon recognize additions or alterations to the painting. Retouching, overpainting or compensation carried out with considerable skill may not be readily revealed to even the expert's eye. It may be necessary to utilize scientific aids to make such determinations.

Many of the past techniques of restoring are considered obsolete today.

'*An Interior with a Woman Drinking with Two Men*' *by Pieter de Hooch (1629-after
1688). Reproduced by courtesy of the Trustees, the National Gallery, London. This
painting is a classic example of pentimenti. The tessellated floor may be observed showing
through the now transparent skirt of the maidservant*

The removal of old restorations provides contemporary restorers with a considerable proportion of their work, since few paintings of age have escaped some form of restoration or alteration during their existence.

OVERCLEANING

All too frequently old paintings show the results of improper solvents having been used in cleaning attempts. Abraded paint, particularly in the thin shadow areas, can have a ruinous effect. Final tints and glazes can be removed in a few short seconds and lost for ever. Strong solvents may continue their penetrating action long after their application.

Attempts merely to clean surface dirt from a painting may also lead to large areas of abraded paint. Some soaps of high lye content can break down a thin varnish film and soften the paint layer. These soaps, combined with a bit of scrubbing, may ruin a picture irretrievably.

OVERPAINTING

The term overpaint is generally meant to describe the application of new paint over original paint.

The observation of ridges or a slightly raised paint level may indicate the presence of overpaint. Scientific aids such as ultra-violet light, infra-red light and X-rays may be needed to make this determination absolute. Lacking specialized equipment, overpainting and retouches may be detected in sunlight.

The network of cracks found in most old paintings is often non-existent or of a different pattern in the overpainted area. The existing craquelure in a painting is obliterated by later paint filling the cracks. This is easily discernible under magnification, which offers proof of overpainting. Areas of a painting showing signs of flaking may reveal themselves as overpaint which has lost its bond to the original paint layer. Further evidence may be found if the style, brushwork or paint texture are inconsistent with the rest of the painting. Overpainting generally indicates an attempt to disguise or cover an undesirable element of the picture's colour or design. Numerous artists have completely overpainted old pictures as an economic measure. The examiner should be aware that some overpaint might be the work of the artist added at a later date.

A picture may pass through many hands in the course of time. Often attempts to tamper with the artist's original conception may be discovered. Overpainting has been employed to add new colours or design to painting compositions occasionally in order to falsify them for increased profit. It has also been used to eliminate parts of the painting considered unfashionable or in poor taste according to period and the individual prejudices of the owner. In addition, overpainting may be applied to cover a multitude of sins. It has been particularly useful in the disguise of abrasions due to overcleaning.

The decision to overpaint a painting today is open to criticism from an ethical standpoint. Some authorities allow a certain amount of compensation where existing photographs (taken before incurred losses) or other paintings by the artist are available for scrutiny. Others regard any suggestion of overpainting as an affront to their integrity. In many commercial restoring firms it is common practice to overpaint. One restorer may repaint only what is still visible or that which the subject clearly indicates is missing. Another may add embellishments of his own choosing. For example, a ship painting might be given flags and rigging never intended by the artist. This is quite modest falsification compared with some.

RETOUCHING

In recent years restoration authorities in the United States have replaced the term *retouching* with *inpainting* in order to emphasize that colour additions should not be allowed either intentionally or accidentally to overlap the original paint. A painting may be examined under the ultra-violet lamp for signs indicating old retouching. Perhaps the supreme attestation of the restorer's skill is retouching which remains invisible to the eye. If the work is carried out by a trained restorer, it will seldom be discovered without the aid of an ultra-violet lamp or accompanying documentation. Artists can appreciate this expertise as most have had to retouch their own pictures on occasion. This often results in larger areas of overpainting than necessary.

Most retouchings of the past are all too visible today. Retouching mediums have darkened and oil paint retouches have oxidized and stand out as defacements rather than carefully matched colours. Long darkened streaks are readily noted on panel paintings where cracks due to warping have appeared in the joins. These attempts at retouching usually overlap the cracks considerably. Darkened retouches which deface the painting or those which were originally ill-matched in colour and tone must be removed to allow for retouching with more permanent modern materials.

The Canvas Support

A canvas support will quickly reveal indications of previous repairs to a trained restorer. Some idea of the artist's concern with future preservation of his work is shown in the quality of the canvas chosen and the methods used in preparing it for painting. Canvas supports of an inferior nature are subject to stress and more vulnerable to attack by atmospheric impurities. A blow that might dent a well-made canvas will tear a weaker one. No canvas is impervious to the ravages of time; some will last more than a century, others less than a decade. Modern restoration techniques, advanced as they are, cannot preserve a painting for eternity. Eventually the paint can no longer withstand the wear incurred by repeated relinings or transfer necessitated by failure of the support.

CONDITION

The general condition of the canvas can be observed for dryness, brittle appearance or sagging. The sagging may be caused by the presence of moisture or loose stretcher keys. Canvas may be worn thin in some areas, exposing the ground. Previous faulty repairs must be removed and replaced. For example, a patch adhered with glue may contract and cause cracks in the paint. Foreign objects such as stretcher keys, wires and nails may lodge in the space at the back of the picture between the canvas and stretcher. These can exert pressure and cause the ground to crack. Accumulated dust in this crevice will absorb moisture, resulting in eventual detachment of the paint. All of these conditions are detrimental to the painting and must be dealt with accordingly.

MARKS

The reverse of a canvas support is exposed to a variety of abuses. Glue labels attached to the fabric have been responsible for contraction of the surrounding area. The pressure exerted by writing with pencil or chalk on the fabric back can cause cracks to appear in the embrittled ground layer of old paintings. Frequently these pressure cracks result in flaking and may in time repeat the mark itself in paint loss at the front. Ink marks or inscriptions may penetrate the fabric and become visible from the front in thin-worn areas. Exhibition and shipping handlers are chiefly responsible for these malpractices. Artists sometimes inscribe various data or titles which should be recorded and photographed during the examination and before lining takes place. The removal of an old lining may reveal marks and inscriptions which have not been documented previously.

TEARS

Tears may be found temporarily secured with transparent tape or cloth tape. Inadequate patches covering tears and holes must be removed and replaced, but broken threads of the warp (vertical strands) and weft (horizontal strands) should not be cut away at this stage.

Not all tears are accidental. Deliberate damage may be inflicted upon a painting for a variety of motives: some political, others social or economic. Usually these outrages are committed by unbalanced persons who want to attract attention to themselves or their cause. The slashing of the Velasquez *Rokeby Venus* by a woman suffragette at the National Gallery in 1844 is an example. Fortunately these slashes were mended with skill that the repairs were left in place when the picture was cleaned and retouched at a later date.

DENTS
Placement of a painting against projecting objects, sudden knocks, or continued pressure from foreign matter lodged at the back are causes of dents or bulges in a painting. If the canvas is weak it may be pierced. In most cases the ground and paint layers are fractured.

FUNGUS
Paintings kept in a highly humid atmosphere are vulnerable to fungoid attack. This appears as fluffy white spores clustered on the surface of the painting. A pocket lens will reveal that they are growing upward through the craquelure. Their appearance at the back of a painting indicates that they are attacking the glue sizing in the fabric support. If left untreated, they will eventually permeate the fabric and destroy the fibres.

Fungus growth, mildew and condensation pose a constant problem for the conservation of art objects, especially in tropical climates. Restorers in these extremely humid areas need special expertise in the treatment of this condition. Australia and India maintain restoration laboratories principally concerned with problems relating to their environment.

ROTTING
The deterioration of a fabric through rotting usually occurs in conditions of excessive humidity. In the past, some books on painting and materials have included the recommendation that linseed oil be applied in order to freshen the appearance and preserve paintings. Unfortunately this treatment does neither; oil darkens and abets fabric rotting.

INFESTATION
Vermin and insects have taken their nibbling toll of fabric paintings stored

for long periods. Mice, ants, silverfish, beetles and moths all find the sized fabric a tasty morsel. Holes will appear in the painting fabric similar to those we find among garments in moth-infested wardrobes.

Linings adhered with a flour paste are prone to termite infestation. The canvas may become riddled with holes as if they were made by pellets fired from a shotgun.

STRETCHERS

The stretcher frame provides an auxiliary support for the canvas. Stretchers are subject to warping, particularly if the dimensions are large and if they have not been strengthened by the addition of a cross bar in the centre. New stretcher frames should replace warped, unaligned or broken ones. Stretchers with sharp edges cause wear to the canvas at the back where it is turned over and tacked. Modern stretcher pieces are usually bevelled to reduce this stress.

Heavy duty staple guns provide an expedient alternative to hammering in tacks when large numbers of canvases are to be stretched. Rusting tacks will affect the canvas adversely. They should be replaced with copper or tin tacks.

A loose or improperly stretched canvas with uneven tension causing rippling may be tautened by tapping in the keys or wedges. The outer dimensions of the stretcher are increased by the intersecting bars being forced apart at the corners. This action is called 'keying out'.

Lining and Relining

A canvas may be lined when advanced structural weakness causes detachment of the ground and paint layers. *Lining* describes the adherence of a new canvas to the back of a failing original in order to strengthen and consolidate the support. The lining process does not involve the thread by thread removal of the old canvas (a popular misconception) but simply the addition of a new canvas to reinforce the old. Paintings are lined as often as it is considered necessary for their preservation. Most Old Master paintings have been lined; some have been relined several times. On the average, a painting may be relined about every seventy-five years. The word *relining* is something of a misnomer as a canvas attached for the first time is really lining the original. Technically relining is done when it becomes necessary to replace the first lining canvas.

It is not always easy to detect a lining in visual examination. The painting must be closely scrutinized at the tacking edges where the canvas turns over the stretcher support to find indications of two separate canvases. A clue to the existence of a lining is the use of paper tape pasted along the sides and turned over the edges at the back of the stretchers.

The Wood Support

The wooden support should be inspected to see if it is a single plank or several joined together. Early wooden panels of large dimension were made by joining planks, thereby precipitating the eventual weakening of the structure as a unit.

Art experts can sometimes provide an approximate date and location for the origin of the picture by identifying the type of wood used in the panel. Even the method of sawing may provide them with information. Occasionally panels were cut down to eliminate unwanted or damaged parts of the painting composition. Additional sections were sometimes joined to the panel later. These were prepared with grounds and compensating paint layers similar to the existing composition. If a dissimilarity in the paint is not immediately discernible, the added wood section itself may be at variance.

The wood may be in an extremely dry condition or it may contain excessive moisture. Dryness may lead to cracking if the panel is in the proximity of severe heat. Prolonged exposure to moisture or soaking of the panel may cause cleavage to the paint and ground. The flood-soaked panels in Florence demonstrated this condition. The initial swelling of the wood loosened paint and ground. As the wood began to dry and shrink, the paint was forced upwards to fracture and cup.

INFESTATION
Insects burrowing into wooden panels can cause the wood support to collapse, resulting in cleavage or fracture of the paint. Panel paintings should not be stored in surroundings where wood-devouring insects may harbour.

DECAY
Mould and decay, generally caused by a damp environment, will weaken and deteriorate the wood support. This in turn has an adverse effect on the ground and paint layers.

WARPING
The chief cause of warping in a panel painting is environmental change. If

kept in conditions of agreeable temperature and humidity, a panel will remain in a state of suspension with little sign of warping or cracking. If the picture is transported to a new locale, warping may be a consequence. The change may cause the planks to separate and fracture the paint surface along the joints. Conversely a panel kept for a long period in a damp atmosphere may warp or split when it is transferred to a dry environment. Central heating has been responsible for a considerable amount of damage to wooden panel paintings, which should not be placed too close to the heat sources.

Early panels painted on both sides have remained relatively stable. The paint has protected the wood from moisture permeation and warping. A similar two-sided protection for contemporary panels is a sound recommendation.

Cradling

A series of wooden slats arranged on the reverse of a wooden panel painting is called a *cradle*. Its purpose is to reinforce the panel and prevent warping. However, when exposed to unreliable atmospheric conditions, the cradle increases the probability of the panel's splitting by not allowing normal movement.

Designed for flexibility, cradles became quite elaborate devices with wooden slats arranged at right-angles to the grain of the panel. The runners, as they were called, were slotted so that they might move in order to compensate for the expansion and contraction of the panel painting. The runners frequently became immobilized, causing the cradle itself to warp, with unhappy consequences to the panel. Cabinet makers of skill were employed in the making of complex cradles. Some of these structures seem equal in craftsmanship to the paintings they back.

Other methods of auxiliary reinforcement involved the gluing of a fabric to the reverse of the panel. Rubens sometimes used this method of reinforcing his paintings with effective results. Additionally, small wedges of wood called buttons were inlaid across the panel joints to prevent separation. Various wooden devices were glued diagonally across the cracks of adjoining planks, all with the purpose of preventing warping. Few succeeded in doing so.

Cradles are still being made for panel paintings when special circumstances warrant. Redesigning of the component parts has in many instances resulted in the considerably reduced possibility of malfunction.

Transfer

When a painting is judged by expert opinion to be beyond the scope of any other restoration process, transfer is the only means of preservation. Transferred paintings are not frequently encountered in the examination of old paintings, although it is an old preservation method.

Briefly, *transfer* describes the removal of the support from the ground and paint layers rather than the removal of the paint and ground from the support as is commonly thought. A more detailed account of the process is given in Chapter VII on Consolidation.

Part II. Scientific Aids

In the light of scientific advancement in the field of fine art investigation, one reads with incredulity some of the advice proffered by leading art authorities and restorers of the past. Modern scientific instruments have provided the means of exploring paintings in depth as never before thought possible.

Scientific apparatus contributes greatly to our knowledge in the field of art restoration. Its successful use, however, is governed by the skill of the person utilizing the equipment and interpreting the information provided.

Scientific advancement often precedes acceptance. Projected theories must be backed with considerable technical data that has been sifted and analyzed. Publication of advanced research in the field of painting restoration is generally confined to a limited audience within the sphere of laboratories and institutions.

PHOTOGRAPHY
Essential to the examination of any painting is the continual photographic record of its condition and of the step-by-step restoration procedures leading to its final completion. Photographs in black and white, colour, normal light and raking light, combined with ultra-violet, infra-red and photomicrography will provide the restorer with complete documentation and evidence of his working procedure. Photographs taken before and after restoration are not entirely adequate.

Photography for painting restoration requires a certain amount of special training. It is important that no falsification is made of the deteriorated condition of the painting or of the completed restoration. Misleading tonal contrasts in the photograph may give the impression that a painting has

'Madonna and Child with St John and Angels' by Michelangelo (1475-1564).
Reproduced by courtesy of the Trustees, the National Gallery, London. An incomplete
work. The figures on the left have been partially underpainted. Unfinished paintings
revealed the artist's methods of constructing a picture before the invention of X-rays

been attacked with a powerful cleanser, making test cleaning strips appear as well-lit windows at night.

Accurate exposures and the dates they were taken, together with complete information pertaining to the condition photographed, are essential data which must be recorded. Future restorers will benefit from this valuable information, thereby ensuring the continued preservation of the painting.

RAKING LIGHT

A tangential or raking light provides a single narrow lightbeam. When the light is nearly parallel with the picture, it exposes any projecting paint rising above the surface. Adjustable desk lamps may be adapted with a directional reflector to give a raking light effect.

Flaking, cleavage, overpainting and even the ridges of another painting composition lying beneath stand out in the bright raking light and contrasting dark shadows. Paint losses and cracks appear as deep canyons. Photographs of impasto brush strokes provide documentation of individual painting styles. The effect of this simple examination may be likened to photographs of the moon with their revelations of mountains, ridges and craters. A photograph taken in normal flat lighting shows little of a painting's true condition; a photograph taken in raking light can be enlightening.

ULTRA-VIOLET LAMP

An invaluable aid to the restorer in every initial examination is the ultra-violet lamp. The rays emitted from the lamp reveal both deterioration in the varnish and alterations by retouching or overpaint whether on top of the varnish or beneath it. The invisible ultra-violet rays are converted by particular substances in the varnish and paint surface to visible lights of different colours. This fluorescence, as it is called, varies accordingly. Varnish usually fluoresces as a yellow-green tone, while overpaint or retouches appear purple, and unvarnished areas in the painting appear a deep purple-brown. Distinguishing a recent retouching on an old painting is made comparatively easy with the aid of the ultra-violet lamp; however, it is more difficult to detect an old retouching.

Ultra-violet photography in colour or black and white may require the services of a photographer who specializes in this technique. Some care must be taken as fluorescence photographs necessitate long exposure and the ultra-violet rays are potentially harmful to the painting. Ultra-violet examination provides useful information about the upper strata of a painting's structure. The accurate interpretation of photographs taken under ultra-violet light is dependent upon the experience of the restorer.

Works on paper such as drawings, etchings and watercolours may be examined under the lamp. Foxing and other forms of paper deterioration, perhaps not yet visible to the eye, will appear distinctly in ultra-violet light.

INFRA-RED

Infra-red photographs provide information concerning the artist's working procedure in the final paint layers. The rays penetrate through grime, varnish, upper paint layers, glazes and tints. Paintings with large areas of shadow may be revealed to have unexpected details or objects not previously discernible. Painters, particularly those of the Dutch school, filled interior scenes with precious detail and then enveloped them in shadow. When the painting was completed, some of the detail was still visible in good light, but eventually the ravages of time and atmosphere wrought changes that darkened the varnish, paint medium and ultimately the pigments themselves. Parts of a low-key composition that have become no longer distinguishable visually are revealed by the infra-red rays. Signatures and faded inscriptions, perhaps lying hidden for a century or more, have been made readable.

Infra-red light is a valuable aid in the detection of copies and forgeries since the rays expose the stages of development in the painting. The copyist can see only what exists on the surface, namely the final brush strokes and glazes. He cannot hope to imitate the painter in depth of artistic creation. He can produce only a superficial facsimile of the original work. His copy, when exposed to the rays, will reveal a feeble foundation of underpainting bearing no resemblance to the original work.

THE MONOCULAR MICROSCOPE

The examination of the strata, pigment particles or cross sections may be conducted with low or high power magnification under a monocular microscope of forty to two hundred times magnification. It is accompanied by a small attached light to illuminate the area of the painting being studied. Photomicrographs may be taken through the microscope by an attached camera. Considerable information may be compiled about the condition of the painting, the grinding size of pigments (fine or coarse) and their dispersion in the binding media.

Quite apart from the technical and analytical study, a world of colourful abstractions unfolds under the microscope. Gold leaf, varnish and glazes dazzle the eye, with fine cracks appearing as canyons and impasto passages as cliffs. These vividly textured fantasies, if blown up to the large scale of some contemporary paintings, would rank as modern masterpieces. Yet the painting under observation may itself be insignificant and the microscopic view may cover less than one half inch of background taken out of context.

THE BINOCULAR MICROSCOPE

Generally less expensive than the monocular microscope, a binocular microscope of low power magnification (ten to thirty times) is extremely useful for closer inspection of the painting. The artist's brush strokes and areas of overpainting are clearly visible.

The binocular microscope may be used for horizontal table-top examination, or it may be mounted on an adjustable stand to scan an upright painting.

POCKET LENS

A pocket lens of six times magnification is a useful accessory for general observation. Lenses of greater magnifying power may be obtained if desired.

BINOCULAR MAGNIFIER

The binocular magnifier is a headband providing stereoscopic viewing which may be used in the examination. It is practical during lengthy retouching as it allows freedom of the hands.

PHOTOMICROGRAPHY

A camera attached to a microscope can be used to record on film, in black and white or colour, the area being studied under high magnification. In addition, photomicrographs may be taken of pigment particles as noted in Pigment Analysis. Detail photographs, referred to as photomacrographs, are usually taken without the aid of the microscope and cover a wider area of the painting. A square inch or two of the painting's surface may be enlarged from two to ten times to record the artist's brush strokes, which appear like furrows in a field. Raised segments of impasto paint and texture are made clearly visible. Painters like Bosch and Bruegel, whose preoccupation with minute details in large compositions is seldom fully appreciated, are ideal subjects for photomacrographic enlargement. A screen projected colour film of Bosch's 'Garden of Earthly Delights' revealed to me many more meticulously painted minute vignettes than I had previously noticed in hours of viewing the painting at the Prado Museum in Madrid.

Isolated details in paintings have not escaped the attention of art book compilers who have, by taking small sections of detail out of context, created numerous individual compositions as pleasing to the eye as a full scale painting. Beautifully illustrated books now appear under titles such as *The Cat in Art* or *Jewelry Through the Ages*, all composed and cropped in the photographic laboratory from detailed photographs of paintings.

STEREOMICROGRAPHY

People who attended the Hollywood stereoscopic films of the fifties will be familiar with the effects created by images in the third dimension. These films proved to have only novelty value and the wearing of special glasses for viewing was a nuisance, yet the basic process, adapted to scientific restoration in recent years, has provided new information. Painting layers can now be recorded by microstereo radiographs which, when enlarged, may be observed through a stereo-binocular viewer.

X-RAY

The preliminary painting examination made with the *ultra-violet* lamp explores the surface by the fluorescent contrasts of varnish and retouching. The *infra-red* rays reveal, in shallow penetration of the paint layers, the artist's changes in composition, obscured signatures and dark passages. Only *X-ray* can achieve complete penetration of opaque paint layers, canvas, ground and support.

The term radiograph refers to the film or plate through which the X-rays have passed. Paint losses and damages appear as dark shadows on the developed film. Repairs, such as patches, filled holes or the shapes of mended tears, are made visible. The condition and grain of a wooden panel will appear and may be identified as to species. The progression and pattern of woodworm bore holes and tunnelling may be assessed.

A disturbing element in the radiographic probe arises when a panel has been coated with paint on the back or has had batons or cradling attached. These are evident in the radiograph and sometimes cause an interference with legibility.

Taking X-radiographs of large pictures may require the use of several separate exposures on single films placed to overlap slightly. When joined, they form a composite X-ray picture the exact size of the painting. Small films can be used to investigate selected areas of the painting and save

see caption overleaf

(*previous page*) '*L'Hiver*' *by Vincent Van Gogh* (*1853-1890*). *The Norton Simon Inc Museum of Art.* (*Below*) *X-ray of a painting of a woman spinning, discovered beneath the Van Gogh painting,* '*L'Hiver*'

expense. The X-ray tube itself is located at the bottom of a lead-lined box. The top of the box is fixed with a glass window through which the X-rays pass. The painting is placed over the window, paint surface upwards. The film is laid directly on to the painting and the X-rays are sent through the back of the picture to register on the film. Often the film resembles the tonal values of the picture. Thick paint in the highlights appears white or light grey. As the paint decreases in thickness and tapers off into shadows, the film registers varying shades of grey. Black appears where holes penetrate directly through paint, ground and support.

For centuries a few written records contained most of our information on the working methods of artists of the past. Except for a small number of unfinished pictures, the actual construction of a painting remained invisible until Röntgen made his discovery of X-rays in 1895. Through the use of X-rays we can now reach into the past to see the preliminary steps in the creation of a masterpiece. Interpretations of radiographic probings may reveal something of the artist's character. Missing stages in the creative process are discovered. We might envision the artist's direct, spontaneous strokes, perhaps slightly hesitating and changing the position of a head or arm, making additions to the composition or later painting out parts that seemed undesirable.

Some paintings are literally X-ray proof. White lead paint in the ground or white highlights impede the penetration of the X-rays. Van Eyck, for example, applied a protective covering of white lead to the back of some of his paintings rendering them opaque to the X-rays. Forgers, aware of the impenetrability of the X-rays to this pigment, have attempted to avert detection by adhering their spurious work on to old supports with an adhesive white lead mixture.

Contemporary works are not altogether suitable for X-ray investigation. The modern picture painted in an alla prima manner is often without layers of stratification, offering little or no depth for the X-rays to penetrate. The actual process of pictorial development is already exposed for examination. Few secrets lie beneath modern works painted with slabs of colour pigment. They are seldom developed with the methodical layer-by-layer construction of previous generations. Individuality in the preparation of supports used by the Old Masters has been replaced by the manufactured wooden supports and mechanically woven fabrics. The X-ray can provide little useful information about the individuality of these modern supports. The contemporary artist might bear in mind that the discarded works which he overpaints to hide from public view may one day be revealed by X-radiography and published for all to see.

Every painting responds individually to X-ray penetration. Repeated tests with rays of varying intensity may be necessary to record on film images that emerged at first as merely indistinct outlines. The timing of the exposure and the development of the film must be repeatedly tested and varied to suit each situation. While X-ray technicians may be trained to do this work, it requires considerable time to develop the knowledge and intuition needed to interpret the X-radiographs of elements within a painting's structure. Only a restorer's experience can guide the technician in determining which parts of the painting need investigation.

Chemical Analysis

The most specialized technology available to the restorer is in the field of chemical analysis. Few restorers have the time or the specific scientific knowledge of chemistry needed to analyse the many components of a painting. Some standard tests, particularly those involving pigments, are of value for the practising restorer. Certainly a working knowledge of the research technician's methods of investigation is an asset to any restorer.

Tests involving chemical and microchemical analyses or experiments with specialized scientific equipment may be applied for compiling data on oils, varnishes, glazes, grounds and supports. Substances added to tint varnish such as glue, vegetable gum or egg protein may be detected. Gas chromatography tests can be made to identify types of varnishes, media and solvents.

Pigment Analysis

Perhaps the most important analytical determination is that of pigment identification and dating. Analysis can prove if a pigment is consistent with the supposed age of the painting. A particular pigment sample taken from a painting attributed to the sixteenth century may be found not to have been invented until the seventeenth century, thus proving it is an addition to the original paint. Information is gained about the artist's methods in the preparation of paints and the chemical changes they have undergone in the course of time. Concentrated interest in this scientific study began in this century. The noted scientist and author A. P. Laurie was a pioneer in this field.

A typical chart for testing pigments may list the following information:
  1. The name and chemical composition of the pigment.
  2. Origin and date of invention.
  3. Particle appearance under low magnification.
  4. Solubility in diluted and concentrated solutions.
  5. Effects of applied heat.
  6. Prescribed reaction tests with chemicals.

PAINT CROSS SECTIONS

The microchemical examination of paint cross sections is a process in which a tiny fragment of paint, often no larger than a pinhead, is imprisoned in a small cube of polyester resin. The cubes are formed in miniature trays. Liquid resin is poured to half fill the tray mould and the paint sample is placed on the fast hardening cube. It is then covered with an equal amount of resin to form a block. A section is then sawn from the resin cube through the paint fragment. Emery paper is used to reduce the sawn section and reveal the tip of the paint specimen for further identification of its stratified layers.

Colour photomicrographs of cross sections containing pigment samples show the paint in sandwiched layers. Fine or coarse colour pigments, translucent glazes, medium and varnish are all recognizable. Ground layers and even a fragment of the support may be included in cases where damage provides a specimen.

I am reminded of a deplorable story related to me by an art professor who, in his youth, decided to make a tour of Europe. Before departing he met an agent of a paint firm who persuaded him to collect paint samples from Old Master paintings. Chemical analysis of paint was then in its early stages.

Armed with a pocket knife and tweezers he visited the leading museums of Europe. Standing before a selected masterpiece, he would await the moment when he was unobserved, then stride to the painting. A minute scrape with his knife was followed by the tweezers grasping the fragment and popping it into an envelope. In this way he collected more than two hundred specimens undetected.

This is a painful story to recall. The professor felt he was providing a service to scientific progress in art. According to him, the paint removals were made from the edge whenever possible, and with skill under the circumstances. I was shocked by his story at the time, and my later experience in painting restoration convinces me his actions were quite inexcusable.

Specimens may be taken from different sections of the same painting to compare original paint with suspected additions by another hand. The removal of these minute samples must, of necessity, be governed by the accepted rule that all original paint is sacrosanct. Detachment should be made with a scalpel under low power magnification. The minute specimen should be taken from the edges or from a damaged area.

Age and Permanency Testing

Restorers and researchers continually conduct tests of new and old materials. Their investigations cover materials used by both the restorer to preserve and the artist to create. A few painting research laboratories carry out experiments following early recipes such as those recorded by Pliny and Vasari. Pigments, varnishes and grounds are prepared in the manner of the Old Masters and studied for behaviour. Various apparatus may be used to carry out specialized tests. The Lovibond Tintometer, for instance, is used to measure the colour variation between areas of the painting before and after the removal of old varnish. Tintometric readings may be obtained by comparing the numerically given colour values with standard colour filters.

Tests are made of pigments, grounds, supports, and natural resin varnishes. Additionally, tests are carried out involving light exposure, flexibility, absorption, strength and resistance. The range of experiments is limitless. The results are usually published in technical journals and many of the findings and recommendations are adopted by restorers and institutions, all of which adds to the vast fund of knowledge exchanged at international levels.

The artist frequently profits from research. A few years ago tests were made in the restoration department of a museum on a quantity of pigment purchased from a well-known manufacturer of artists' materials. An undesirable substance, which would have adversely affected the pigments, was extracted in a large lump. A report was made to the manufacturer with a request for an explanation. The embarrassed directors of the firm apologized and assured the museum that it would not happen again, and the offending element was eliminated. This kind of co-operation helps to ensure that established standards in the manufacture of artists' materials are maintained.

CHAPTER VII

CONSOLIDATION AND REPAIRS

Part I. Paintings on Fabric

Consolidation is the term used to describe the process of re-attaching paint with adhesives by flattening the separated layers of flaking or cleavage, and the reinforcement or replacement of damaged or deteriorating fabrics and panels. Specialists sometimes undertake the work of consolidation, particularly when it involves the vacuum lining or transferring of paintings for preservation. Many restorers find that the expensive equipment and the time consumed in these operations limit the amount of work they can accept. The laying of detached paint is a procedure normally carried out by restorers and involves a minimal amount of equipment.

The surface of the working table is prepared prior to carrying out any treatment. A large blanket of felt or soft cloth is used to cover the table and to provide a cushion for raised impasto areas of the painting. The cloth is covered with a transparent Melinex sheet (polyethylene terephthalate) or Mylar which is the US equivalent. This covering does not readily stick in the presence of heat. The table should be kept free of any tools or objects which may hamper the work in progress.

Surface Protection

Before most consolidation operations can begin, the paint surface should be faced. *Facing* a picture means applying a protective paper or fabric to the front to prevent damage during treatment, transport or storage, and to hold loose paint particles in place. Not all pictures need to be faced; it depends entirely upon the condition of the structure and the particular treatment contemplated.

The most commonly used facing for a small, thinly painted picture is a single layer of tissue held by paste. A larger painting may require several layers of paper or cloth and adhesive to secure the paint. Wet-strength tissue and Japanese mulberry paper are best suited for this purpose. The long fibres of the latter provide considerable strength. Papers prone to wrinkling and contraction while drying should be avoided.

This sensitive seventeenth-century portrait of Michelangelo suffered paint loss during the Florence flood. Sheets of facing tissue secure the loosened paint

Paintings with sound structures are sometimes cleaned before the facing is applied. Loose or cupped paint is flattened to ensure a smoothly affixed facing and to prevent additional damage during application, treatment and removal.

A strong facing may be necessary when the picture to be treated has areas of deep cracking or impasto paint, or when it is to be transferred. The facing may be in the form of heavy cloth, paper, or plaster casts fashioned to protect the ridges and depressions of impasto paint from the pressure of flattening and lining. Fabric facings are seldom required unless a picture is to be transferred.

The type of adhesive employed is largely determined by the operation to be performed. It must be soluble in solvents which do not affect either the surface coating or paint layers. A paste facing may be used over resin paint and resin facing over a water-based paint. Beeswax, wax-resin mixture, polyvinyl acetate, thermoplastic synthetic resins and normal butyl methacrylate are used for non-aqueous facings. The prerequisite for any facing must be that it is easily removable.

PASTE FACING

Paste facings may be used when work such as wax-resin treatment is contemplated. The wax-resin adhesive melts when heat is applied and would be of little use in securing the paint during these operations. Water soluble (aqueous) paste, starch or glue mixtures are employed to adhere the facing. Varnish is not usually removed as the paper has a tendency to shrink and pull when drying. Recipes for facings are numerous, but the main consideration should be that they do not shrink and cause damage to the paint. Some restorers recommend a paste facing recipe consisting of wheat flour of the white, non-rising variety mixed with water. A few drops of formaldehyde are added as a preservative if the paste facing is to remain for a long period. Cellofas B, mentioned in Chapter IV on Paper, is another useful facing adhesive. The dampened paper is brushed separately with paste and carefully laid on the paint surface, followed by smoothing out any air bubbles by hand. When the facing has dried it affords the paint protection for as long as may be required.

Removal of a paste facing is effected by dampening the paper with warm water. The paper is loosened at the edges and torn off slowly in strips pulled away parallel to the picture surface so that any paint flakes not fully attached may be discovered before lifting.

Faced areas containing wax that has been used to treat flaking may stick and need to be removed by dampening with white spirit before peeling. Paper that begins to disintegrate may be gently rubbed and rolled off. Free of the paste facing, the picture surface is sponged lightly with a small amount of warm water. A soft cloth is used to absorb any remaining moisture which could prove damaging to the picture's structure.

WAX-RESIN FACING

A wax-resin facing may be made from the same ingredients used for lining paintings. but with varied proportions. A warmed mixture of four parts beeswax with six parts dammar resin dissolved in a small amount of turpentine or white spirit provides a suitable facing preparation. The greater proportion of resin is employed to reduce the flow properties inherent in the wax. The adhesive is warmed and brushed through the facing paper which is placed in direct contact with the paint surface.

The facing is removed with a light application of white spirit, which loosens the paper and aids in detaching it. A wax-resin facing is not normally used on a painting when heat is to be applied through the back of the canvas as in the wax lining process.

Reattaching Loose Paint

FLAKING

The flaking of paint generally takes place in the paint layer with the ground often remaining intact. However, paintings severely affected in both the paint and ground may have to be lined. Further flattening may be necessary after the lining operation as this alone is not always sufficient to secure flaking completely.

Some restorers find it preferable to clean paintings before re-attaching and flattening paint in order to permit better adhesion and relieve the surface tensions created by the varnish. Cleaning is not advisable when loss or fracture of the paint may occur because of an advanced condition of flaking or cleavage.

The adhesive used for paint flattening may be gelatine size with certain paintings and grounds or the same wax-resin formula that is employed in the lining of paintings. Both the ingredients and the proportions of the wax-resin may be varied considerably depending upon the individual condition under treatment and the personal preference of the restorer. The waxes may be of synthetic manufacture or natural beeswax. Resins may be synthetic Keytone N or natural dammar. A typical recipe might advise a mixture of seventy-five per cent beeswax and twenty-five per cent dammar resin. The preparation is heated in a double boiler and stirred until melted and blended.

During the operation to lay flaking, the canvas must be supported underneath. A heated electric spatula (preferably thermostatically controlled) is held over the area of flaking with one hand while a lump of wax held in the other is pressed against the tip. A few drops of melted wax are guided to the detached paint area. A small isolating sheet of Eltoline tissue or heat resistant silicone paper is then placed over the drops of wax to prevent the heated spatula from coming into contact with the paint. A sheet of transparent Melinex can be substituted for the tissue. This permits close observation of an area in order to avoid damaging, cupping or flattening impasto paint. The heated electric spatula is moved in slow circular motions slightly above the flaking to warm the paint prior to applying pressure. Warmed by the heat, the wax begins to melt and flow under the tissue. The wax is worked back and forth into the cracks. The continued pressure and slow movement of the spatula flattens and fuses the paint. The spatula can either be allowed to cool during the final stages of this operation or may be replaced by an unheated one to ensure adhesion.

A cloth dipped in white spirit is gently rubbed over the tissue to remove the permeating wax. The protecting tissue is gradually removed from the wax by pulling a corner back slowly, parallel to the surface. If resistance is encountered, a little more white spirit on the wax holding the tissue will relax it. Excess wax remaining on the paint surface may be wiped away with cotton wool dipped in white spirit. A hand-held electric hair dryer is useful for slowly melting the wax on the surface, facilitating its removal. If the paint is not satisfactorily flattened and adhered, the process is repeated.

CLEAVAGE

Cleavage describes the loss of adhesion between the support, ground, or paint layers. *Buckling* is the overriding or ridging of the paint over a section of cleavage. Extensive cleavage or buckling of fabric paintings is best dealt with by lining. Works on wooden panels exhibiting this condition in an acute form may have to be transferred . Small areas of cleavage may be corrected in the same manner as flaking, by laying with a spatula using wax-resin or size. Several applications of wax-resin may be required to penetrate fully beneath the cleavage and permanently secure the paint. Infra-red lamps are useful in keeping the wax-impregnated area warm and pliable while flattening paint with the spatula. Small irons are sometimes used to flatten large areas of cleavage.

Wax paper or Melinex, blotting paper, a rubber mat, hardboard and weights are placed over the treated area to secure the paint. If the flattening is not entirely successful, the process is repeated.

Successful attempts have been made to inject adhesive into the cracks with a hypodermic syringe. This allows penetration of the crevice under the area of cleavage. Another method recommends lifting the detached paint sufficiently to allow a fine brush, filled with adhesive, to be inserted into the void. Obviously a steady hand is required in this manoeuvre as there is a risk of totally detaching the paint.

BLISTERING

The treatment of blisters is dependent upon whether the blister is brittle as the result of age or intense heat, or whether it is flexible as in the case of fresh paint. Satisfactory results have been reported in adapting a vacuum hot table to lay fire-blistered paint.

Large blisters are prepared for flattening by the injection of a gelatine solution with a hypodermic syringe. The injection may be made either at the base of the blister itself or by careful penetration from the back of the canvas into the blister hollow, taking care not to pierce the dome. The latter method, if carefully conducted, is particularly suitable for brittle blisters, as there is no need to puncture the fragile paint.

Panel paintings, of course, cannot be treated by injection from the back. Consequently, brittle blisters should be protected beforehand by application of a durable wax gently brushed or dripped over them to prevent splintering when the needle is inserted. The puncture itself may be made with a sewing needle that has been heated red hot and inserted, thus burning a tiny hole which provides access for the hypodermic needle.

Once the adhesive has been injected into the blister, tissue is placed on top and a warm electric spatula is passed slowly back and forth over the blister without quite touching the paper. This allows the size and paint to warm and fuse before direct gentle contact is made. Only slight pressure is needed to adhere the blister to the ground and support. The flattening is continued while the spatula slowly cools to obtain the best results. A less fragile blister or blisters in recently applied paint may be laid by heat, tissue, wax-resin and gentle spatula pressure without a syringe injection.

WRINKLING

A slight wrinkling in the paint may respond to treatment by simply passing

A patch applied to secure a tear on the reverse of the canvas has shrunk and appears as a depressed area

a warm spatula back and forth over the tissue-protected area with increasing pressure. This action will work only if the distorted paint still has the plasticity provided by the oil which was originally responsible for the wrinkling.

Tears and Punctures

The mending of tears and punctures that will escape detection is a skilled operation. If the repair has been incorrectly made, the outline will be visible on the front of the painting.

Fabric patches applied to a tear at the back of the picture were not always successful. They often had a tendency to shrink upon drying, making the repair visible and causing distortion to the canvas. Patches are applied to a torn canvas with a similar piece of fabric of slightly larger dimension than the void. The threads at the edges of the patch are pulled and frayed or chamfered so that the edge is thinned and the patch will not appear as a shape on the front of the painting. Thermoplastic adhesive or wax-resin is applied with an iron to affix the patch to the back of the picture. The tear is then ready for filling and retouching on the front.

Tears or punctures are frequently found in old canvases, particularly if they have never been lined. In most cases, the lining operation will serve to secure them. Before the canvas is lined, the tear is flattened and the frayed edges are trimmed and aligned. Old patches or mending tape that have been used temporarily are removed. Extremely large tears may necessitate the canvas being bonded to a rigid support.

Holes and Perforations

Paintings may be encountered with part of the picture torn away and missing. A complete loss such as this must be reconstructed by replacing the missing fabric, ground and paint layers. To accomplish this, a piece of fabric similar to the support in weave, number of threads, conformation and weight is required. It must be slightly larger than the lost area.

The piece of patching canvas is laid on to a cardboard-protected table and the painting is placed directly on top of it so that the hole is centred. A scalpel is used to cut around the edges of the hole through the underlying patching canvas. The frayed threads of the hole are trimmed and the patch, which is now cut to the dimension and contour of the hole, is removed and coated with a plasticised polyvinyl acetate. A second piece of canvas for backing is also coated with the PVA and both are allowed to dry.

The painting is placed face down on a sheet of heat-resistant silicone paper and the patch is inserted into the hole and properly aligned. The reinforcing canvas is placed over the patch so that the two PVA coated sides are joined. A domestic iron set at a medium temperature is used to heat and melt the thermoplastic PVA and form a bond. The patch is finally secured and ready for filling and retouching.

The Purpose of Lining

Pictures are lined when a fabric support has deteriorated to the point that the paint and ground may be endangered by loosening, cracking or flaking. Paintings should be lined before these conditions are advanced.

The continued preservation and survival of most old paintings today is due to the process of skilful lining. Pictures have been lined and relined for centuries. Lining, as previously described in Chapter VI on Examination, means the adhering of a new canvas to an old deteriorated one. Relining means removing an old lining canvas and replacing it with a new one.

Glue Adhesives

Early linings were attached with glue, glue with paste and other combinations, or a mixture of white lead and linseed oil. The latter adhesive is particularly difficult to remove and it also absorbs X-rays, making the film illegible. Glue was destined to be replaced for most lining operations by a more stable wax adhesive. Nineteenth-century Dutch restorers were among the first to use the now standard wax lining process.

Glue linings do not effectively bond paint and ground. They are now used less frequently than the more thoroughly penetrating and easily removable wax-resin. Glue is generally used if cleavage and cupping are advanced, or if a pigment such as bitumen will be affected by heat. Glue starch compounds and cold setting glue are among the most popular for lining purposes.

Glue is subject to attack by mould and it is vulnerable to dampness which causes swelling. Upon drying, it is apt to shrink, with ultimate damage to the paint structure.

Perhaps the most stable aqueous adhesive is a water emulsion of polyvinyl acetate applied in several thin coats to the lining fabric to prevent sudden shrinkage. Unfortunately it has only limited penetrating power.

Wax-resin Adhesive

A wax-resin mixture is used both for adhering a lining and for paint re-attachment. The normal lining recipe consists of six parts beeswax to four parts dammar resin melted together and applied while hot. Colophony is often used as an inexpensive alternative for the dammar. Variations of this formula and proportions of the ingredients may be necessary on occasion.

There are several advantages in the use of wax-resin for lining. The most important are the flexibility of the infused support and the low melting point of wax, which makes future removal of the lining easier than with any other adhesive. Wax forms a protective barrier against moisture and air pollution. Paintings lined with wax should not be exposed to heat or the direct rays of the sun. Conversely some pictures lined with wax have fared better in hot tropical climates than those lined with glue compositions which are more susceptible to insect infestation and mould growth.

Lining wax passing through the canvas is said to have a discolouring effect on paintings which may alter their appearance. This discolouration is infinitesimal on oil colours but tempera paintings may be slightly more affected. There is concern about the slight darkening of some Impressionist and modern works lined with wax-resin. Unlike most paintings of the past, these often have exposed areas of ground or thinly painted colour. Darkening of the ground may disturb the harmony of colour relationships. To alleviate this problem, bleached waxes and clear resins can be used in the lining mixture.

The Removal of Old Glue and Wax Linings

Before an attempt is made to remove an old lining, the picture is faced to withstand the tension. The picture is placed face down and the glue lining is separated from the original fabric at one corner. The old lining is peeled from the original fabric in strips and the adhesive is scraped off.

Glue that is in a brittle condition responds well to scraping or abrading. If it is not brittle, it is softened by a little moisture and heat before the fabric is detached and the adhesive scraped. Remaining glue is carefully sanded with a fine sandpaper so as not to abrade the fabric threads. The dust is brushed off and the fabric cleaned with white spirit on cotton wool. Old adhesive left on the canvas will obstruct the passage of the new molten mixture.

Removing an old lining canvas in strips to prepare the picture for relining

Wax linings are removed by melting the wax with an iron, or remelting the whole area on the hot table and peeling the fabric gently. White spirit is used to loosen the wax and ease removal.

Preparation for Lining

The painting to be lined for the first time is cleaned of all surface dirt. The varnish is removed, unless it is in a sound condition, so that hard accretions will not damage the paint when under ironing or vacuum pressure. Some restorers say that if the varnish is removed a new coat should be applied to protect the paint before facing; others consider this unnecessary.

The painting may be faced with an appropriate adhesive, taking into consideration that a picture to be wax lined cannot be faced with wax or it will melt. If the picture has ridges of paint or impasto, a mould or cast facing may be required to protect the paint from the pressure of ironing. Mending patches are removed from the back and any marks or inscriptions are recorded. A painting may be lined with a transparent synthetic fabric, called a surfacing veil, which permits notations of historic interest to remain visible.

A new lining canvas of greater dimensions—a few inches longer and wider than the painting to be lined—is tacked on to a loom which is a stout version of the stretcher frame without expandable corners. The thickness and weave pattern of the lining canvas should be consistent with the original support. For example, a thick lining should not be adhered to a thin original canvas. Some restorers recommend that the lining canvas should be soaked before stretching to alleviate further shrinkage should the picture come in contact with excessive moisture.

The painting is removed from its stretcher by taking out each tack carefully. It is not cut away from the stretcher as the turning edges are conserved for as long as possible. The painting is placed face down on a table protected by a sheet of Melinex. The back is inspected for any protrusions, such as knots or loose fibres, which are cut away. The two canvases are then ready to be joined by ironing or vacuum hot table lining with appropriate adhesives.

Wax Lining by Ironing

The oldest method of lining a painting is with an iron. In the past, heavy irons were used which cooled rapidly and needed heating over fires.

(Above) Lining a painting with an electric dry mounting iron and wax-resin; (Below) removing excess wax-resin from a painting lined by ironing

As a result of their weight, many of the linings that had been performed with an iron fractured the paint and rendered areas of high impasto completely flat. Several paintings by Rembrandt exhibit this condition to a marked extent.

Today the use of special electric irons and ordinary light household irons fitted with an additional metal plate allows greater control of both heat and pressure. Lining with an iron can be accomplished in a limited space with a small amount of equipment.

The painting to be lined is placed paint surface downwards on the prepared table. It is brushed on the back with the hot wax-resin mixture that is gently spread with a heated iron. The loom-stretched lining canvas is placed over the back of the picture and held by weights, if necessary, placed at each corner. Liquid wax is applied evenly to the back of the loom-stretched canvas with a stiff brush in a Union Jack pattern from the centre outwards. The consistency of the wax is workable but not so fluid that it runs.

The electric iron is kept just hot enough to work the wax into the fabric, infusing both canvases. It may become necessary to add more wax if the canvas is highly absorbent. The area covered is not more than a square foot at a time. The heated iron must be kept moving so as not to damage the picture underneath. This process is repeated in the adjacent area and continued systematically, working from the centre to the outer edges of the underlying painting. Both canvases must be fully impregnated and fused or there will be a lack of adhesion. The wax must flow to the edges of the pictures and extend to the lining canvas overlap to ensure complete bonding.

Any areas not properly bonded are gone over again. The electricity is then shut off and the ironing continues while the iron cools. A lasting adhesion takes place when the wax has cooled and set.

A hard coating wax may be applied to the back of the newly lined picture, creating an additional moisture barrier. The picture is finally cut from the loom and tacked back on to its original stretcher, if it is in good condition, or on to a new one.

Hot Table Vacuum Lining

Another method of wax lining employs an electric hot table with an element-heated metal top and a vacuum pump for extracting air. A hot table is an expensive piece of equipment and not every restorer owns one.

A thermostat-controlled hot table with vacuum pump for lining paintings

They are a most valuable asset when lining pictures with marked brush work or textured surfaces. Unlike the iron, which places the heaviest pressure on raised paint surfaces, the vacuum method distributes the pressure evenly over high points and depressions, thereby preserving delicate sections of paint.

A lining canvas prepared for the vacuum operation is stretched on the loom just as it is for the ironing process. The lining canvas is brushed with the hot wax-resin mixture and then cut away from the loom at the edges so that the overlap is retained.

The lining is laid on a large sheet of Melinex in the centre of the hot table. The painting, also impregnated with wax-resin, is placed face up on top of the lining fabric, bringing the two waxed sides together. Another sheet of Melinex is laid over the painting to form a sandwich. Strips of canvas or felt are placed like a frame round the edges of the Melinex sheet. These form tunnels which serve as vents for extracting the air through holes at the edges of the metal hot table. A latex rubber sheet is laid over the assembled layers. This is held in place by metal bars or weights which form the layers of material into an envelope to trap the air. The heat and vacuum pump are switched on and a thermostatically controlled heat is produced in the metal table top. The surface temperature is maintained at about 52°C as indicated by a table thermometer placed on the covered painting. The vacuum pump acts to extract the air from between the paint surface and the membrane, channelling it out through the canvas strips leading to the small holes at the table edge. The removal of the air brings the Melinex and rubber sheet into vacuum pressurized conformation with the picture surface. At the point when the wax has melted sufficiently to penetrate and fuse both canvases, the heat is turned off but the vacuum pressure retained until the table has cooled, allowing the wax-bonded fabric to set. The pressure created by the vacuum is kept low enough to avoid imprinting the canvas texture into the paint.

Wax forced through holes or tears on to the paint surface is cleaned away with white spirit. The lining overlap is trimmed and the painting is retacked on the original stretcher, if it is in good condition.

STRIP LINING

A canvas support in relatively good condition may have weakened or splitting areas at the point where the canvas turns over the stretcher edge. Sharp-edged wooden stretcher frames and tension are usually the cause of this condition. Reinforcement with strip lining provides adequate protection without lining the whole picture.

In this method, strips of raw canvas the dimensions of the picture and two to three inches in width are cut and chamfered at the edges and attached with adhesive to the back of the painting. They are turned over the stretcher edges extending no further than the inner edge of the painting covered by the frame. The wax-resin lining mixture may be used to hold the strips, which must be kept under weights until completely adhered to the canvas.

An old stretcher frame with sharp edges should be replaced or the edges rounded with a sanding block. Modern stretcher pieces are usually bevelled on one side. Care should be taken when fitting them together that the edges correspond. When the canvas is restretched, it is placed on the bevelled side of the stretcher and tacked at the back.

MAROUFLAGE

The French term *marouflage* is used to describe the bonding of a fabric to a rigid support. Painters often do this to strengthen thin fabric materials. The advantage is a canvas painting surface with a fully protected back.

Restorers who marouflage fabric paintings to a rigid support take care to use adhesives that will facilitate safe removal in the future. Too often untrained persons use the same concoction of glue simmering in the pot that they have been using previously to join frames. How the same person might set about the eventual removal of a painting that has been adhered in this manner is a sobering thought.

Part II. Paintings on Wood

Many of the methods of consolidation and preservation used for paintings on fabric may be employed on wooden panels. An obvious exception is that treatment cannot be carried out through the back to consolidate layers on the front of the picture.

Wooden panel paintings are faced and the paint flattened in the same manner as on fabric. Paintings on wood are not lined in the sense that a new fabric secondary support is provided. Rigid reinforcement or transfer is necessary to stabilize a wooden panel that shows signs of excessive warping, cleavage or infestation. In the past it was common for panels to have additional wooden cradles or metal cleats attached to provide stability.

Flattening Warped Panels

Possibly the greatest defect of wood as an otherwise suitable long-lasting painting support is its tendency to warp. The correction of warping has often resulted in further damage to the panel and paint. Force should never be used to flatten warped panels. Warping is usually due to a loss of moisture in the wood which causes shrinkage. The panel can be temporarily relaxed by placing it in a damp atmosphere. Light weights or books may be placed on the paper-protected surface at the apex of the bow. The weights may be gradually increased over a period of days until flattening is maintained after they are removed.

It is not advisable to rehang the picture in the same atmospheric conditions which have been instrumental in causing it to warp. Installation of hygrometric equipment might, in certain instances, be justified to maintain a check on humidity. This is somewhat impractical unless a valuable picture or collection is being protected.

A truly satisfactory method of flattening panels permanently has yet to

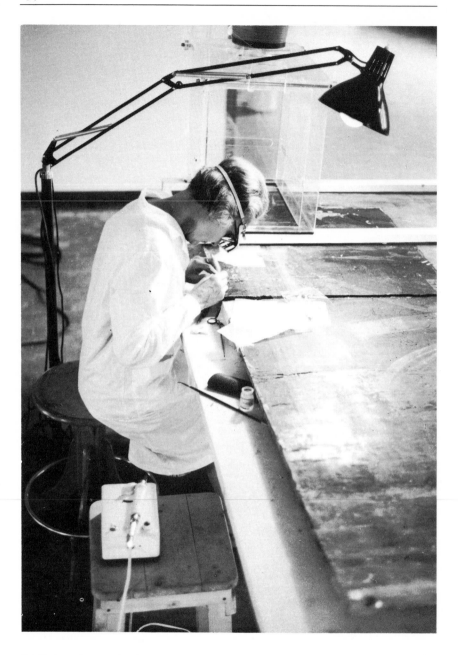

Replacing minute paint fragments on a panel. The restorer wears a binocular magnifier. In the foreground is a thermostat-controlled electric spatula. A perspex fume extractor is in the background

be devised. Impregnation of the wood at the back of the panel with glycerine has been tried with limited success.

Many years ago I helped in the installation arrangements for an exhibition of Old Master landscapes in the art gallery of a California college. The work was on loan from several mid-Western and Eastern collections. Three days after the exhibition opened it was noted, with considerable alarm, that a crack caused by warping had appeared in a small Brueghel panel and in another Old Master painting on wood. The exhibition was immediately disbanded and the pictures sent back to their owners. Once returned to their previous environment, the warping discontinued.

Although the college gallery was kept under humidity control it was evident that the paintings had been affected during shipment to a dry climate. The arid conditions caused dehydration of the wood on the reverse side, which was unprotected by paint. Wooden panel paintings invariably contract towards the unpainted side. Panels painted on both sides are less likely to be affected by warping. This is a point worthy of consideration by contemporary artists.

Cracks in Wood

A small crack developing in warp-affected wood may ultimately result in the complete splitting of the panel. When this occurs, the separated edges are inspected and cleaned. The picture is placed face up and both edges of the crack are thinly coated with an adhesive such as epoxy resin. They are then joined together under pressure by clamps fitted to hold the outer edges of the panel until the adhesive dries. Excess adhesive which has been forced from the crack is removed with warm water and cotton wool swabs. A waxed paper, rubber pad and light weights are placed over the join so that the panel will not buckle from pressure exerted by the clamps. The panel is left to dry in this vice arrangement until secure.

Cracks and cavities in the wood surface are filled with gesso or putty. Cavities on the reverse side may be filled with a wax filler containing such inert materials as china clay or powdered chalk.

Cradling

Cradles were devised to prevent the warping and splitting of wooden panels. As previously described in Chapter VI on Examination, the cradle is usually made from hardwoods attached by glue to the back of a panel painting in a construction resembling lattice work. A series of wooden strips are placed at regular intervals, parallel to the panel grain. These strips are slotted to allow for a second series of strips, not attached by glue, to be intersected through them.

A cradle is attached to add mechanical strength and to prevent the panel from warping, while at the same time allowing for expansion and contraction. In practice, cradles have generally caused more damage than they have prevented. The moveable parts can jam, restricting the normal movement of the wood and inducing splitting in the panel or flaking and cleavage in the paint. Any signs of warping or cracking will necessitate removal of the cradle from the panel.

The most permanent way of stabilizing a picture and eliminating warp and further cracking is not by the addition of a cradle or cleats but by total replacement of the wooden support itself in an operation called transfer. Sometimes a painting support may be strengthened by the partial reconstruction of the existing panel.

(Left) A modern oak cradle. (Right) A nineteenth-century mahogany cradle

Removing the facing tissue from a panel painting which has split under stress

Reconstruction of a Panel Support

Damage to panels, such as that caused by woodworm or accidents, may require only a partial reconstruction of the panel rather than complete replacement. The outer wood of the panel is reduced to within one-eighth of an inch of the ground with a wood plane and chisels. A linen fabric is then attached to the back with wax-resin to provide stronger adhesion between the original panel and the composite support to be added.

Balsa wood is sometimes used as a new support for transferred paintings as well as a reconstruction material. Its lightness in weight is particularly advantageous for large paintings.

The basic step of creating a new backing support involves cutting balsa wood into strips. One method recommends that strips be cut three to five inches long, depending upon the size of the picture, and about two inches wide, from a one half to one inch thickness of balsa wood. A wax paste mixture for binding the sections is made from beeswax, with china clay, chalk and fine sawdust as inert filling materials. The wax paste mixture is brushed on to the back of the fabric previously affixed to the panel. A hot lamp is used to soften the wax and then removed for a short period to allow setting. The sections of balsa wood are soaked in melted wax-resin, brushed with the wax paste on the joining edges and then pressed on to the fabric. They are set in rows in staggered sequence, similar to laying bricks, parallel to the panel grain. As each section of balsa wood is pressed into place, the cracks between are coated liberally with wax paste and pressure is applied with small weights until the wax hardens.

When the first layer has been fixed and the wax set, gauze strips are laid to cover the back. A second layer of balsa wood pieces are placed across the panel grain perpendicular to the first layer in the same manner as previously described. Excess adhesive is scraped away and the panel is allowed to dry and is smoothed with a wood plane. The edges and corners are rounded by sanding. A heavy linen is then cut to cover the back and overlap the edges. This is ironed on with wax to complete the panel. The final result is a strong lightweight panel that is protected from moisture.

Transfer

The transfer of paintings refers to the removal of the paint layers and occasionally the ground from one support to another. A French restorer, Picault, revolutionized restoration by being the first to transfer to canvas a painting which was originally on wood. Several canvas-to-canvas and canvas-to-wood transfers took place in the eighteenth century.

When relining is no longer sufficient to secure flaking and deterioration, it may be necessary to transfer the painting to a more stable support. Contrary to popular belief, transfer of paintings is not a sensational process by which the paint is miraculously skinned from the ground and support to be re-attached to a new panel. The decision to transfer a painting is the result of much careful deliberation and is reached only when all other means of stabilizing the picture have been exhausted. Paintings exhibiting extensive cleavage or weak and brittle fabric supports are likely candidates for transfer. The operation is time-consuming and must be undertaken with extreme care and skill.

The method of preparing a panel for removal is preceded by the application of one or more layers of heavy facing. Layers of facing paper followed by a layer of fabric are applied to protect the paint from stress. Restorers in Florence used the hard film-forming paraloid B72 (soluble in xylene) to secure paper facings for transfer. A fabric was then adhered over the paper with a heavy coating of gesso to form what might be described as an inverted temporary support for the paint and ground during the course of transfer.

In the first stages, a heavy wooden support is removed mechanically by using an electric circular routing saw or an electric plane. The planks are further reduced with hand planes, gouges, and chisels to within one-eighth of an inch of the ground.

The use of power-driven tools may seem unwarranted but in the case of large panels they are indispensable. Many panels in Florence measured several feet across and six or more inches thick. They were usually battened with large wooden timbers, which added a cumbersome weight so that several men were needed to move them.

Small knives are used to remove the remaining layer of wood to reveal the ground. Sometimes the condition of the ground may necessitate its complete removal as well, which requires weeks of painstaking work. The paring down is a process in which light sanding of the hard *gesso grosso* ground may be permitted initially, followed by the scraping of the softer *gesso sotile* ground to powder with a scalpel to within a fraction of the paint itself. Only a small area is covered at a time. Then a new ground of gesso is prepared and brushed on in thin, even coats. A fabric of nylon mesh or muslin is imbedded in the gesso. A sheet of paper fibre board is used to hold the back secure in preparation for transfer to its new support.

Composite Supports

There are numerous types of composite wooden supports for transferred paintings. A composite support has the advantage over natural wood of not having directional grain that is subject to cracking. Plywood, box board and various machine-pressed boards have been used with success by restorers. Sundeala, a rigid lightweight board, is an excellent support for paintings.

In addition to wood, metals such as aluminium have provided supports for smaller pictures. The comparative resistance of metal to stress is an advantage. Plastics in various forms have been tried, with limited success, but experiments are continuing. No doubt the chemical laboratory will provide a wealth of materials to choose from in the future.

Since World War II, a few paintings at the National Gallery in London have been transferred to a honeycomb composite support. As the name implies, cells resembling those constructed by bees are made from resinated paper. The size of the cells is variable. The honeycomb is sandwiched between two Sundeala boards glued with epoxy resin and backed with a fabric as a moisture barrier. This provides a reasonably lightweight support for the transferred paint layer.

Infestation Control

Insects infesting panel paintings may be exterminated by fumigation with poisonous gas or impregnation of the panel by brushing or spraying liquid insecticides. Carbon disulphate is an insecticide for fumigation which will not affect paint. Although safe for paintings, it is not advised for use by the untrained, as carbon disulphide fumes have explosive properties when mixed with air. A sealed gas chamber is required for this work and precautions must be taken against smoking or exposed lights.

A number of liquid insecticides are available for use. Advice from specialists should be sought before purchase regarding their possible detrimental effects on paint. Care should be taken that the chosen mixture does not harm paint by softening or staining and that it will not damage gold leaf or gesso if they are present. After testing, the liquid may be injected directly into the bore holes with a syringe. Spraying is relatively ineffective for insects that are deeply burrowed into wood. Bore holes themselves are not necessarily an indication that insect larvae are still active.

After treatment, the boreholes may be filled with beeswax containing some of the insecticide. The wax is melted with an electric spatula and allowed to fill the tunnels. If the holes are properly filled, an inspection made in a few months' time should reveal that no fresh insect activity has taken place.

MOISTURE BARRIERS

Paintings on wooden panels and composite boards can be protected from moisture penetration by a linen fabric adhered to the back. Any cracks and cavities are filled beforehand with a wood-filling compound.

The linen is cut sufficiently large to overlap the panel. Wax-resin is brushed on the back and edges of the panel, then spread uniformly with a heated iron. The fabric is laid on the panel and wax-resin is again brushed on evenly. The fabric is ironed from the centre to the edges, which are attached with a heated spatula for easier control.

A hard coating of microcrystaline wax is rubbed on the fabric and then polished with a chamois leather to create a durable moisture barrier. The wax is also effective in keeping the back free from dirt.

CHAPTER VIII

CLEANING PAINTINGS

The cleaning of paintings is seemingly one of the easiest tasks that faces the restorer. The operation involves only a minimal amount of supplies, most of which are readily available. Therein lies the greatest fallacy. The possession of equipment is no guarantee of successful cleaning. All cleaning is hazardous and the expert is the first to acknowledge this. Cleaning is perhaps the greatest test of a restorer's judgment and ability. One can never predict the cupidity of varnishes and paint films.

Few masterpieces have survived earlier restorations unscathed. Subsequent cleaning may reveal abraded paint layers or paint previously skinned by strong solvents. Some of the methods used in the past seem almost barbaric. Paintings have been subjected to maltreatment of all kinds, including washing with urine, acids and ammonia. They have been abraded with sandpaper and set alight, crepe suzette fashion, using alcohol to burn off decomposed varnish. Attempts have been made to regenerate old varnishes by long exposure to brilliant sun or by rubbing onion or potato slices over the surface. Such homely recipes should be labelled housewives' tales. They can actually be most harmful if any of the vegetable juices penetrate through the cracks to the priming.

An old recipe from the De Mayerne manuscript of 1620 reads as follows: 'Thoroughly rub and soak the oil painting with soft soap and a sponge. If it is very dirty, let the soap stand on it for a while. Afterwards, wash with urine and rinse with water, throwing it vigorously against the picture. In the beginning the water must be warm, later it can be thrown on from a bucket.'

Paintings have literally been scoured away by the industrious application of soap and water in the hands of their owners. When works have been only lightly varnished or not varnished at all, treatment with soap and water can remove layers of paint. A picture was once brought to me by the owner who had attempted to clean it with a household cleanser. In a few minutes the damage wrought by this action had greatly reduced the value of the picture.

Cleaning may be more appropriately called *devarnishing*, which describes the removal of the varnish coating by solvents, vapours or by mechanical means such as rubbing or scraping. Cleaning is accomplished in separate stages, beginning with the removal of surface dirt, then varnish and finally old retouchings. Some restorers strip both the dirt and varnish layers in one operation, although the preferred procedure is to undertake them in separate stages.

The appearance of colours is altered by darkening varnish. Some are deepened in tone but remain still recognizable, while others are rendered indistinguishable. The veil of darkened varnish and dirt completely obscures true hues while the underlying paint itself stays nearly as bright as on the day it was first applied.

During cleaning, the restorer must be constantly aware of the artist's original intention in his colour relationships. While some pigments have undergone changes, others have remained stable, resulting in misleading tonal contrasts. A picture in which the pigments have darkened due to the use of excessive amounts of balsams and essential oils is beyond successful restoration. The removal of an old varnish will, in this instance, lighten the colours considerably, but as the pigments themselves have been affected, total restoration cannot be achieved.

Cleaning twentieth-century paintings is extremely hazardous due to the solubility of new pigments. In a short time oil pigments appear dry but because of additives such as oils, varnishes and painting mediums, they can take from thirty to seventy-five years to evaporate and harden completely. Recent or unhardened paint can be dissolved by even the mildest solvents.

The reaction of a painting to cleaning is unpredictable and tenuous. Each picture presents a new test of the restorer's aptitude and experience. Many factors are involved in the skilful cleaning of paintings. Experience must be complemented by an intuitive feeling for each individual painting and the particular problems it may present.

Protective Picture Varnish

Picture varnish provides a transparent protective coating against dirt and grime without unduly discolouring the pigments. In addition to affording protection against minor abrasion, varnish must be flexible enough to allow normal movement of the support.

Varnish enriches colour tones and intensifies the contrast between light and dark colours, creating an illusion of greater depth.

Paintings may be varnished with more than one varnish of dissimilar composition. For example, a painting may be coated with a spirit varnish and at a later date with an oil varnish; thus several coats may be accumulated over the years. Further applications of varnish are often applied with the erroneous notion that they can revive obscured colours. Initially this treatment appears to be effective; later the new varnish becomes a further obscuring film.

A common practice amongst eighteenth- and nineteenth-century artists was the addition of warm toned colours in the varnish mixture to give pictures a fashionable patina of age and a cherished golden glow. Sometimes artists who copy paintings with overlying yellow varnish do not realize that the colour tones they are so intent upon imitating are not those of the pigments applied by the artist but those created by the filtering varnish.

There are two principal types of picture varnish: resin dissolved in a volatile solvent (spirit varnish) and resin dissolved in a drying oil with thinner added (oil varnish).

Spirit varnishes are composed of soft resins, such as mastic or sandarac, dissolved in alcohol or turpentine. They are generally brittle and can be removed from pictures with comparative ease.

Oil varnishes, made from hard resins such as copal or amber, are melted in oil at high temperatures. These varnishes are hard and durable, resisting most solvents of moderate strength.

Types of Resin

AMBER is a fossil resin found in the area of the Baltic Sea. It is most familiar as jewelry in its natural state. Amber was seldom used by itself as a picture varnish because of its slow drying and dark appearance. It has often been confused with copal. Amber is impervious to many cleaning solvents.

COLOPHONY (ROSIN) is the residue remaining after the distillation of spirits of turpentine from the balsam exudes of various pine species. It is used with harder varnishes to increase their fluidity. Colophony is not suitable as a picture varnish by itself, but it is sometimes employed with wax as an ingredient in picture lining.

COPAL is a hard resin. Varieties of copal are obtained principally from fossil resin found beneath the earth. It has been used infrequently as a picture varnish since the Middle Ages. Copal is generally hard, darkens with age and becomes nearly insoluble. One of its principal uses was as a high gloss varnish for coaches.

DAMMAR resin is considered to be the most popular picture varnish for paintings. Dammar is obtained from trees in Malay and the East Indies. It is the most durable and transparent of the soft resins.

MASTIC resin is derived from trees grown principally on the Greek island of Chios. Mastic has been used extensively as a picture varnish, often with additives to increase its elasticity. It becomes brittle and yellow with age and is vulnerable to bloom in a moist atmosphere.

SANDARAC comes from a coniferous plant grown mainly in Africa and Australia. Sandarac was frequently used as a varnish ingredient in early paintings. It tends to redden with age.

SHELLAC is a tree insect secretion of a resinous nature. India is its principal source. Shellac is sometimes used as a primer for wood supports, since it prevents resin from penetrating through and affecting the paint film. It is impervious to nearly all solvents used on oil paintings. Shellac has seldom been used as a picture varnish.

Varnish Regeneration

In 1870 Max Pettenkofer, a chemist at the University of Munich, published a book which described his patented process for restoring the surfaces of oil paintings without endangering them. Briefly, the process involved placing a picture with ageing varnish into a box containing alcohol vapours. The resin varnish was fused and rendered transparent after exposure. The intention of the process was not to remove the varnish but rather to make the picture more visible. The Pettenkofer method, as it is known, was used on several pictures in the National Gallery with apparent success and many restorers still consider it valid for the rejuvenation of aged varnish.

The process is used to reduce or fuse craquelure and partially to reduce wrinkling, bloom, blanching, and overall dullness. It softens and re-forms obscuring varnish film by exposure to solvent vapour. The process recaptures some of the picture's original lustre. Unfortunately it will not remain this way for as long a period as would a new coat of varnish, but it does improve the picture considerably.

Solvents

The restorer uses a variety of solvents in the cleaning process. The usual approach is to start with the mildest solvent and work up to those of greater strength.

It would seem that a weak solvent would be the choice to ensure safe cleaning but this is not always the case. A weak solvent may require prolonged treatment, allowing it eventually to penetrate and soften the paint film. A stronger solvent may, on the other hand, dissolve the varnish, which is then removed before it can affect the paint. A fast-acting solvent is particularly suitable for pictures with weakened ground and paint structure, which should be cleaned with as little swab manipulation as possible. Intense concentration and decisive action are required when using all solvents.

Strong solvents used for varnish removal may necessitate haste and invariably old varnish remains in the hollows between the ridges of impasto paint or the threads of a rough woven canvas. Painstaking efforts with a pointed brush, dipped in solvent, or a scalpel, are needed to remove this varnish residue.

Slow-acting solvents cause the varnish to swell and form a gel. The rate and degree of swelling varies between solvents. The more volatile or quick-evaporating solvents tend to act faster.

A method of cleaning by spraying solvents is occasionally used on hard varnishes. A strong solvent is sprayed over a small area in a thin mist. This serves to soften the outer varnish layer. The remaining varnish may be removed with a swab dipped in a weaker solution, reducing danger of penetration through to the paint.

The solubility rate of varnish and paint films differs widely. Sometimes one varnish will react to only the strongest solvents while another can be dissolved by the weakest solutions. Because paint solubility is always uncertain it is treated initially with the caution afforded new paint, although it may ultimately prove hard enough to resist strong solvents.

There are as many complicated recipes for cleaning solvents as there are restorers to implement them. A few of the more involved mixtures sometimes demonstrate a bit of showmanship. It is not always necessary to use a mixture of solvents; often a single solvent will accomplish the task.

The experienced restorer is able to select and test the correct solvent from an extensive list. Among the most commonly used solvents are ammonia, cellosolve, ethyl and methyl alcohol, toluene, turpentine and xylene. Two of the most popular solvents are probably acetone and isopropyl alcohol. Both are diluted with white spirit as required.

Diluting agents such as white spirit have little dissolving effect on old varnish films but are capable of softening more recent varnishes.

Some solvents may prove to have ill-effects on the person using them. Skin or eye irritation, respiratory ailments, dizziness or headaches may affect the restorer. Work with solvents should be carried out in a well-ventilated room. Solutions of a toxic nature should always be handled with care and in the presence of functioning fume extractors.

An excellent source of reference for the physical properties of solvents and dilutents can be found in Gettens and Stout's *Painting Materials*.

Surface Cleaning

The amount of surface dirt on pictures varies with their surroundings. Pictures kept in a clean air environment will accumulate less surface accretions than those exposed to industrial soot and grime.

The patina of the ages has been increased by industrialization. A few years ago I visited Florence while the cleaning of the Duomo was in progress. Three artisans were at work on a scaffold suspended along one side of the edifice, where the marble had been cleaned to its natural brilliance, a striking contrast against the area of grime. While admiring a completed section, I noticed that a creeping film of oxidization had already begun to obscure the lustre of the Carrara marble. It is likely that by the time the workmen had completed their circuit they would need to begin again.

Pictures are affected by atmospheric impurities in much the same manner. Surface dirt should be removed with the same care as picture varnish, since many cleaning agents are capable of removing varnish as well as dirt. Dry cleaning should precede wet methods. Dust must be removed by light brushing with a feather duster or soft cloth. Not all dust can be removed, a good deal remains in the varnish where it had accumulated before the varnish had dried. Additional layers of varnish have often been added over the previous dirt-covered layer in an attempt to revive the colours. These only contribute to the further obscuring of the painting and the embedding of dirt. Some restorers claim that a synthetic detergent and water are comparatively safe for cleaning surface dirt from pictures, provided that the ground is bound in oil and a stable varnish underlies the grime. The liquid, spread with cotton wool formed into a pad, is not allowed to remain on the surface longer than to effect removal. Another cleaning solution sometimes used is the combination of a few drops of ammonia and lissapol in a quart of water. Restorers occasionally employ the alkali content of saliva to aid in cleaning dirt accumulations. When surface grime has been removed from a heavily incrusted picture, the visual effect is often equal to that of old varnish removal.

Unvarnished paintings are particularly susceptible to abrasion by cleaning agents, and restorers exercise extreme care in cleaning these surfaces. Apart from contemporary works, old tempera paintings are the principal unvarnished pictures likely to be encountered.

Four experimental sequences of test cleaning a print
1 *Original state — dirt and stains ingrained*   3 *Spray applications of chloramine-T*
2 *Dry cleaned*   4 *Immersed in sodium hypochlorite*

Cleaning Preparations

There are numerous commercial preparations manufactured to surface clean paintings. Some of them are fairly safe and will remove dirt adequately. Others are dangerous, although the advertising insinuates they will remove surface dirt like a miracle kitchen cleanser. Unfortunately they may have the same effect on varnish glazes and paints as the cleanser might have. A few manufacturers assert their preparations will clean, preserve, revive varnish and remove bloom in one operation. There has even been talk of a do-it-yourself picture cleaning kit including a variety of solvents and step-by-step instructions. Restorers and art lovers will blanch at the thought of the incalculable damage such a kit might cause.

Many people surmise that picture cleaning preparations can be used to take off varnish as well as dirt and vigorously rub the surface when they find the varnish resisting their efforts. Winsor & Newton, the well-known suppliers of artists' materials, have issued the following cautionary instructions in the pamphlet describing their product for picture cleaning:

WINTON PICTURE CLEANER

Directions for use:

1. Remove the oil painting from its frame and lay it flat on a table.

2. Shake the bottle of cleaner vigorously to mix the contents thoroughly. The emulsion must be uniformly white and creamy before it can be used. Shake the bottle every time you want to apply cleaner to your pad of cotton-wool.

3. Moisten a wad of cotton-wool with the cleaning emulsion.

4. Apply to the surface of the painting by means of a gentle, circular motion. Never allow liquid to remain on one part of the surface. Keep the cleaner evenly distributed over the whole area.

5. Take a fresh wad of cotton-wool as soon as the old piece becomes dirty. Repeat the process as long as necessary to achieve the desired result. Remember that some time will be required for the essential oils to penetrate the hardened varnish, and that the exercise of patience will be well rewarded. Never rub hard and be sparing with the amount of cleaner used.

6. Stop the cleaning immediately if colour is observed on the cotton-wool.

7. When no more dirt is brought off on the cotton-wool, the painting

should be wiped over with fresh cotton-wool moistened with English Distilled Turpentine.

8. The surface will now be slightly tacky. Put the picture aside in a warm dust-free atmosphere until the surface has rehardened. This may take a few hours.

9. If considered desirable the picture can be re-varnished with Griffin Picture Varnish or, when a less glossy effect is required, with Winton Matt Varnish.

Testing

No one method of cleaning is appropriate for all paintings. Each picture has its individual problems which are determined by testing. In most instances, cleaning tests are begun with weak solvents which evaporate quickly. If the varnish proves insoluble the strength of the solvent is gradually increased until the varnish attains a removable gel state. A slow-acting solvent might continue its action and soften the underlying paint before it is removed. The restorer conducts careful tests to find a solvent containing properties that will soften the varnish without penetrating and dissolving the paint. The edges of the picture, previously covered by the frame rebate, may show some evidence of the original paint colours.

Varnish removal tests are usually begun over impasto areas and light colours such as clouds or flesh tones that are usually less vulnerable than shadow areas which may be made from pigment in varnish glazes. The minor areas of the painting are tested before important passages. Tests are generally made in rectangular strips of about two or three inches in length.

There are few infallible methods of cleaning paintings. Each painting reacts differently to solvent action; areas of the same picture may respond quite differently. No one solvent or group of solvents may be said to be safe for cleaning a painting until positive tests have been made.

The Technique of Removing Varnish

Before a picture is cleaned loose paint is flattened and re-attached so that varnish removal is made easier and safer. The surface grime is cleaned and the picture is ready for devarnishing.

Good light is essential for the cleaning operation. Restorers prefer either an evenly distributed daylight or artificial light. The picture is preferably placed on an easel in a vertical position. Cotton wool dipped in white spirit is

Cleaning tests on an eighteenth-century portrait

sometimes wiped over the area to be cleaned immediately before the solvent is applied. This not only affords the restorer better observation of the area but also aids in diluting the solvent slightly and reducing its strength. It usually has little effect on either the varnish or paint films of old pictures.

Solvents and dilutents are stored in stoppered containers. When needed they are poured into a beaker or small glass jar. Swabs are made of cotton wool wound on to a stick. They may be purchased ready made in medical supply shops where they are sometimes called 'applicators'. The swab, dipped in solvent, is rolled gently back and forth between the thumb and forefinger on the varnish, avoiding abrasive friction.

Cotton swabs are not rubbed nor pressure exerted to clean tough, resistant varnish. The swab is constantly examined after each application for any sign of colour or loose paint fragments. As the swab becomes dirty, the cotton wool is replaced.

A second swab dipped in a restraining agent is held ready. The restorer must be prepared to apply the restrainer if there is any sign of the solvent overacting. Appearance of colour on the swab is the signal for cleaning to be stopped immediately. Any solvent remaining on the picture is completely absorbed by cotton wool so that it cannot damage the paint. Bright primary colours such as reds, blues and yellows are more easily discernible on the swab than umbers, browns and blacks which are difficult to distinguish from varnish. Shadows painted with these pigments were often applied in resinous glazes. It is difficult to differentiate between these glazes and the brown varnish. In such instances the restorer may rely as much on his sense of touch and sound as on his sight.

The action of a swab on varnish creates a smooth sliding sound to the practised ear, while a harsher sound is audible on original paint. The feel of varnish on the end of the swab is oily and sticky; on original paint it feels drier. It takes constant practice over many years for the restorer to develop this high degree of sensitivity.

Paintings with deep cracks are cleaned with considerable care. If the surface is allowed to become too wet, the solutions may penetrate through the structure, loosening the bond between the paint layers. Impasto paint may be caught by the cotton wool and particles broken away. A long-haired varnish brush may prove of assistance when high ridges of paint are encountered.

Old and brittle varnish films are easily scratched. The slight pressure of a finger rubbed across it is sufficient to disintegrate the varnish. In this degenerated state, it may be removed by a method of friction rubbing.

Mastic varnish responds to friction treatment more favourably than other varnishes. A small amount of resin is placed on the finger-tips and rubbed in a corner of the picture causing the old varnish to disintegrate. The removal technique has limited application and it is sometimes difficult to determine if all the old varnish has been removed.

In the past partial cleaning was sometimes attempted if complete cleaning was judged unsafe for the painting's structure. A few restorers practised this method when removal of the varnish might have revealed old overpaint or paint losses necessitating lengthy retouching. Others tried to leave a vestige of old varnish so that the paint tones remained mellow. Partial cleaning techniques were seldom wholly successful.

Today total cleaning is recommended so that all traces of old varnish are removed. The ultra-violet lamp is useful for fluorescing varnish remaining after the cleaning operation. Occasionally spots may be left untouched by the solvents used to clean a picture. These blemishes may be foreign matter, quite unlike the varnish removed, or the residue of previous varnishings. Scalpels or razors are sometimes used to remove the particles. Restorers, with the skill of surgeons, take great deliberation when using sharp instruments on paintings.

Blanching and Bloom

During the process of cleaning an oil painting, areas of greyish opacity called blanching may appear on the surface after the solvent has dried. Blanching is the result of a powdered precipitate of the varnish left as residue. Solvents which may cause this condition tend to be those having a rapid evaporation rate such as acetone or solvents miscible with water.

A dilute solution of cellosolve in white spirit has been effective in dispersing blanching. Other suggestions for treatment range from feeding the blanching with linseed oil to scraping away minute particles with a scalpel. The use of linseed oil in this manner is somewhat unreliable as the paint could become slightly darkened.

The application of a small amount of distilled water gently rubbed with a soft cloth will often disperse bloom on sound varnish. If the varnish is in an unsound condition necessitating its removal, the milky opaque bloom will be completely eradicated at the same time.

Mildew

Mildew or fungus growing on the back of paintings on canvas can be

(Opposite) 'Portrait of the Painter in Old Age' (detail) by Rembrandt (1616-1669). Reproduced by courtesy of the Trustees, the National Gallery, London. A fine example, after cleaning, of a painting with impasto brushwork. The varnish has been removed with great care as rough paint texture impedes removal of varnish from the depressions. (Below) a nude by Anders Zorn (1860-1920), a Swedish painter. Photographed during the varnish removal

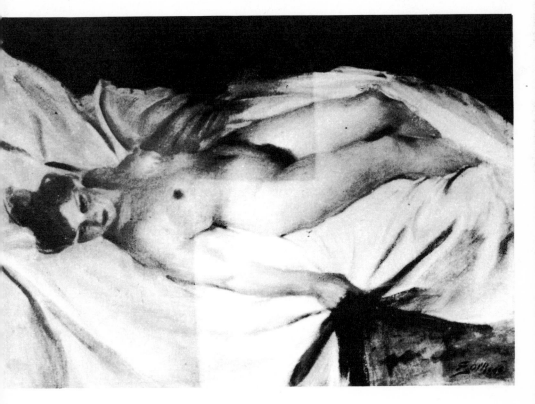

treated with a fungicide if the material has not already begun to rot. The mildew spores should be lightly brushed away. A weak solution of about 5 per cent formaldehyde should be applied by gently brushing. If a large area of the reverse of the fabric support has been affected, an atomizer may be used to spray the formaldehyde lightly. Short periods of exposure to sunlight are beneficial following this treatment.

Detection of Overpaint during Cleaning

Grime and discoloured varnish may cover the tonal differences existing between darkened overpaint and the lighter tones of original paint so that they are not visible during examination. Cleaning will reveal these to the trained restorer. Suspected overpaint must be examined thoroughly. If there is any doubt that it is a later addition, no attempt is made to remove it as the possible loss of original paint is too great a risk.

Additional paint may be detected when it appears on top of a previously repaired area of damage. An overpainted passage may vary in hardness. It may be softened by a cleaning solvent which has left original paint untouched, or it may prove insoluble to solvents capable of removing original paint.

REMOVING OVERPAINT

Old retouchings darken with time. They often extend over original paint and stand out as unsightly paint blotches. Attempts have been made to remove darkened retouches by simply overpainting them. The restorer must remove these layers before he can begin proper restoration.

Retouchings, overpaint or varnish which are insoluble with the normal solvents are softened by an ammonia-wax paste applied for a few minutes, then removed. Some retouches or small areas of overpaint are eliminated by scraping with a scalpel under a magnifying glass. Recognizing and removing overpaint are tasks which only a skilled restorer should undertake.

Separating Paintings

In the past when X-rays revealed a painting of possible significance under-lying a visible picture, a decision had to be taken either to remove the top painting, thereby destroying it, in order to expose the picture underneath, or to leave it hidden forever. During the last few years, a Greek restorer and icon specialist, Stavros Mihalarias, has been a leading figure in perfecting a revolutionary technique for separating and preserving paintings that have been executed one on top of the other.

The actual details of the separation process remain undisclosed to all but a few. However, the basic concept is that a piece of silk is adhered to the paint surface, and special solvents are used to penetrate slowly through the painting on top to soften the varnish lying between the two pictures but not beyond. The solvents are alternately applied and removed by drying. At the optimum moment the upper painting is gradually pulled away intact on the silk support. There is no single method applicable. Every case is individual and must be treated in a separate manner with a variation in the solvent application.

Naturally some risk is involved in the excruciatingly delicate separating process. Mr Mihalarias spends a considerable amount of time in research and testing until he is convinced the operation will be a complete success. During the actual separating operation the painting undergoing treatment requires constant supervision which may last for many hours.

Unknown paintings, many of which may have been hidden for centuries, may be revealed in the future. The possibilities opened up by this new technique are inestimable. In one instance three icons on one panel were separated, resulting in a new legacy for the art world.

The separation of some modern paintings which have been overpainted within a short space of time has recently been achieved. Their separation is usually dependent upon whether the original picture has been varnished. The art world is just now becoming aware of this seemingly impossible feat. Museums, dealers and collectors are studying the reports with increasing interest as X-ray examinations continue to detect hidden paintings. After all, no owner could object to having two Picassos for the price of one.

Controversy

The science of restoring pictures is not new; restoration has been practised since the earliest days of painting, although it remained for centuries an undeveloped science. A few learned artists and scientists foresaw the potential need and left valuable manuscripts recording artists' techniques and the evolution of restoring methods.

The rapid advance of restoring techniques has, as in many other technical fields, left all but the experts behind. It is no wonder then that the hue and cry of critics is heard when a famous picture is slated for cleaning. Critics are usually extremely knowledgeable about art techniques and history but they are not always aware of the advancements in restoration processes. Controversy serves a useful purpose by focusing attention on the restoration and preservation of art which is the heritage of succeeding generations.

The National Gallery

The National Gallery in London has long been one of the world's leading institutions in the field of scientific investigation of the treatment of pictures. A policy has been instituted to keep the public informed in matters pertaining to pictures in the collection. Proposals to restore important pictures and reports on the progress of the work are often made public. The 1947 exhibition of cleaned pictures illustrates this policy. Smaller exhibitions displaying methods of cleaning and transfer have been staged during recent years.

The world's leading art institutions have begun to allow the public closer scrutiny of the achievements of their restoration departments. The administrators of the National Gallery policy obviously believe that an informed public is in a better position to appreciate the advancement of restoring techniques and potentialities.

Currently the restoration of important pictures at the National Gallery is being carried out by the eminent restorers Mr Arthur Lucas and Mr Kenneth Malcolm, who are continuing the programme of public enlightenment. The pictures in the collection are inspected every eight weeks. Over one hundred are treated each year in two large well-equipped restoring studios. Unless pictures are being restored or on loan, the entire collection of more than two thousand pictures is on public view. It is interesting to note that many of the world's great galleries display only a part of their collections, literally the tip of the iceberg.

The administration of the Gallery is aided by a committee of Trustees appointed by the government for a period of seven years. The committee meets once a month to discuss policy and restoring schedules. A painting under consideration for treatment is brought before the Director and Trustees. A summary of the painting's history is given by the Chief Restorer, who may outline preservation proposals. The Trustees may include eminent artists, historians or economists, in fact, members of many professions who have shown a concern for the art heritage of the nation.

The National Gallery issues a bi-annual report describing the individual condition and treatment of works undertaken during the period.

THE 1947 CLEANED PICTURES EXHIBITION

During World War II, the paintings in the collection of the National Gallery were evacuated to the country accompanied by two restorers who continued the cleaning policy already instigated. In 1947 the National Gallery opened its doors on one of the largest exhibitions of cleaned and restored paintings ever assembled.

If the administrators had been aware of the debate that was to rage for years to come, they might have presented the newly cleaned pictures individually over a period of time. A gradual presentation might have allowed viewers to become accustomed to the startling tonal changes and bright colours that were in complete contrast to the former mellow amber tones. The complete display set the scene for a long bitter controversy.

The exhibition caused considerable discord among the art critics, academic painters and art historians on one side and the Gallery administrators and restorers on the other. Letters between the adversaries were exchanged in leading newspapers and journals. Some correspondents thrived on the personal publicity the controversy achieved while others were motivated solely by their love of art. Many people expressed their views but few had bothered to speak with qualified restorers. The artist Sir Gerald Kelly advocated a cautious procedure of varnish removal stopping short of the last thin layer. He demanded an investigation of the alleged drastic cleaning methods. In principle, he and other informed critics were not opposed to cleaning in some form.

Among those who clamoured for the support of an investigation were Augustus John, Sir Alfred Munnings, Rodrigo Moynihan and many others. Particular paintings in the exhibition were cited as having been ruthlessly overcleaned, including Rembrandt's 'Woman Bathing' and Rubens's 'Chapeau de Paille'.

Supporters of the National Gallery's view included Professor A. P. Laurie, the noted restorer and author; Albert Houthuesen and artist Duncan Grant, who wrote an open letter on behalf of other signatories.

The debate continued and ultimately a fact-finding committee was appointed to investigate. Under the chairmanship of J. R. H. Weaver, the committee sifted through the facts and made their recommendations to the Trustees. The report of the Weaver Committee served to instigate vast conservation reforms both in the United Kingdom and abroad. As a consequence of these reforms both the conservation and scientific departments of the Gallery were expanded.

Restorers still suffer unjustly from the criticism levelled at them during the 1947 exhibition. I was speaking with an Italian restorer in Florence when I had occasion to mention the fine work being done in the National Gallery restoration laboratory. He countered with obvious disdain: 'Have you *seen* the overcleaned pictures in the National Gallery?'

'BACCHUS AND ARIADNE'

In an earlier period in the history of restoration, the Raphael cartoons underwent such drastic retouching they provoked a lawsuit in 1738. A more recent controversy involved the cleaning of Titian's 'Bacchus and Ariadne', which suffered considerably from flaking. In May 1967 the National Gallery issued a press release announcing a decision by the Trustees that cleaning should be undertaken. Public statements on decisions of this nature are seldom made, but in this instance account was taken of the numerous admirers of the picture. A clamour of conflicting opinion was evoked regarding the suitability of their recommendation.

After their own examination and before implementing their plan, the Trustees, acting on the report of the Chief Restorer, Mr Arthur Lucas, decided to appoint a learned international committee to investigate and advise on the proposed methods of treatment. By establishing such a committee, they hoped to placate those expressing concern, but a few were not so easily persuaded and the controversy continued. The now impeccably restored 'Bacchus and Ariadne' hangs as a testimony to the competent and skilful restoration at the National Gallery.

CHAPTER IX

RETOUCHING AND REVARNISHING

A painting by Rubens depicting Aesop's fable *The Lion and the Mouse* hangs in the British Prime Minister's country house at Chequers. According to former Prime Minister Harold Wilson, during Winston Churchill's World War II residence there, the great man, unable to see the mouse properly, took up his brush and retouched it. When Mr Wilson was asked if he would attempt to improve the mouse, which was still rather faint, he replied, 'I wouldn't touch up a Rubens, still less a Rubens touched up by a Churchill.'

Examples of retouching have occurred throughout art history. Occasionally the retouching has been the work of the artist himself. More often it has been made by another hand in an attempt to add new elements or obscure existing passages in the composition. Considerable retouching has been done to suit the taste of the period, the dealer or the collector. Apart from aesthetic considerations, retouching was intended to improve a picture's sale potential. It may have been carried out expertly by a restorer or quite crudely by an amateur.

Today informed opinion regards paint losses (lacunae), abrasions or other damage to the picture surface as the only areas which justify retouching by anyone other than the artist who created the painting. All original paint is considered sacrosanct even though it may at times be less pleasing than the retouching.

The reasons for retouching are numerous. In the past a sense of moral indignation was the reaction to nudity depicted in certain works. To placate the offended critics works of art were retouched with drapery, foliage, shadows or other disguises. In our more enlightened times most of these additions have been removed so that the works may be seen as they were originally intended.

Typical illustrations of morals and retouching are Michelangelo's paintings in the Sistine Chapel. Outraged church officials demanded the addition of modesty veils to the nude figures. The artist summoned to add these embellishments became known as the 'Pants Man'. He was one of a legion of minor artists employed in the task of covering up offending paintings and statues during an age of prudery. From this group of artistic specialists one might establish a new title, 'Master of the Fig Leaf'.

The figures in the Sistine Chapel have been restored to their original state. A sign in the Chapel requests that visitors refrain from lying on the floor in order to view the ceiling. Vendors of rental mirrors circulate among the throngs of sore-necked tourists who find difficulty in staring rapturously upwards for long periods of time.

The terms retouching, inpainting, repaint, and compensation are sometimes used by restorers in similar connotation; yet subtle distinctions exist. Retouching and inpainting embody a similar activity but inpainting is felt to describe more clearly that the paint is kept strictly within the perimeter of a paint loss. Repaint indicates that a missing part of the design or a larger area of paint loss has been replaced. Compensation implies that reconstruction of a missing area of the design is carried out with an awareness of the artist's original intentions. Overpaint is, as the term describes, additional paint applied over original paint.

Deceptive Retouching

The delicate skills of the restorer are rarely fully appreciated by the art-gallery visitor. The work on the reverse of the painting is not visible and repairs or retouching on the front are, when at their best, undetectable. What a shocking sight the same pictures would present if they were left unrestored. Displayed 'before' and 'after' photographs of restored paintings often attest to the startling transformation.

Retouching is one of the most demanding tests of a restorer's ability and skill. The perception of a painter is a considerable asset in this work. There is much controversy in the art world as to whether a painting should be retouched to deceive completely or whether the retouching should be done in neutral tones, allowing the viewer to observe the missing areas. Some restorers believe that only original paint is permissible and that damage should merely be toned so as to avoid interference with the aesthetic appreciation of the picture. The ethics of retouching are a matter of constant concern to the restoring profession.

Reconstruction

Reconstruction may be described as repainting that portion in the design of a picture which has incurred paint loss. The restorer should not attempt to repaint areas when there is insufficient evidence of the original design. Reconstruction should be based only upon known factors. Preliminary drawings or existing copies of a work are invaluable in showing the complete composition design for reconstruction purposes. The restorer is aided by photographs taken prior to the damage. By studying photographs, for instance, it would be possible to reconstruct the extensive areas of paint loss in the Cimabue crucifix, which was badly damaged in the Florence flood. For aesthetic reasons, however, repainting the Cimabue is not contemplated.

Filling Paint Losses

Before retouching is begun, the areas of paint loss must be filled with a putty. Filling may be described as the insertion of adhesive material into a crack or cavity in the ground to bring it almost level with the painting surface. Old retouches which have altered are removed and in most cases it is necessary to remove the filling as well.

Gesso mixed with chalk, gypsum and size is a traditional filling. Putty filler recipes may include the basic components of gilder's whiting mixed with rabbit skin glue and a few drops of linseed oil to form a pliable mixture. The putty is coloured with pigments to match the original ground. It must have elasticity and dry without shrinking. A number of commercial wood filler preparations that will adhere indefinitely to either panel or canvas are available. The putty is normally worked into the void with a small painting knife. Any overlapping putty is gently rubbed away with a piece of silk dipped in distilled water.

TEXTURING THE PUTTY

While the putty is still pliable, a simulated canvas grain texture can be imprinted. A mould impression of a similar type of canvas may be made for this purpose. The putty is given a light varnish coat to reduce absorption and to isolate it from the pigment layers to be applied. Without the canvas weave impression or a similar texturing of the putty, the retouched area, no matter how well colour matched, will appear flat and shiny, quite unlike the surrounding original paint. The filling is left fractionally lower than the surrounding paint surface so that the retouching will blend invisibly.

Retouching Media

A properly retouched paint area should resemble the original paint in colour, texture, transparency and gloss. The newly added retouching must be stable enough to resist damage or changes of colour. It must adhere to the surface of the picture firmly yet the medium should be readily and safely removable by solvents should this prove necessary in the future.

The choice of an ideal paint medium for retouching generates a divergence of opinion in restoring circles. Several schools of thought exist regarding the suitability of one medium over another. The debate over whether or not oil colours should be used for retouching oil paintings and tempera for tempera paintings continues. Restorers are united in their opinion that there is no ideal retouching medium for all purposes.

The most commonly used retouching media include oil, oil-resin, wax-resin, watercolour, tempera and the recently developed paraloid B72 which is a synthetic resin. It is unlikely to darken or crack, permitting tones to be matched directly with little allowance for colour changes upon drying.

Most restorers agree that dry colour pigments should be employed. Many modern pigments are too finely ground by machine to correspond with old pigments ground by hand. The coarser particles of hand-ground pigments in old paintings must be imitated to achieve a similar texture in the retouching paint. Matching textures is as important as matching tone. A smooth texture will appear noticeably out of character if the original paint is more coarsely grained than the addition.

Pigments ground in oil have proved unsatisfactory for retouching. The oil darkens rapidly and it is difficult to imitate the look of old original paint. Attempting to retouch paintings with tube oil colours is not advocated today as commercially prepared oil paints do not have the properties necessary to ensure that the retouching remains in harmony with the original paint.

Watercolour bound with gum arabic and tempera bound with egg, both traditional painting media, have perhaps the best compound qualities required for retouching. Both are handled with reasonable ease. They remain quite stable and, if properly applied, are removed without undue effort.

Colour Matching

A retouching which extends beyond the perimeter of the damaged area

'The Virgin and Child' (detail) by Masaccio (1401-1428). Reproduced by courtesy of the Trustees, the National Gallery, London. Darkened retouching appears on the Madonna's robe and on the Child's feet

usually may be attributed to an earlier restorer who attempted to blend his colours with the surrounding paint. The escalation of retouching may have been taken to the extreme in some instances. Some small museums have adopted the policy of letting contemporary artists whose work they possess retouch their own pictures, which can result in gross overpainting.

An artist who is untrained as a restorer may not be competent to retouch even his own paintings. For example, a contemporary artist noticed a fleck of paint on the sky area of a newly painted landscape. Instead of leaving it to dry and flicking it away with a knife point, he tried to remove it with a little turpentine. He then had to retouch the larger spot made by the solvent and eventually he had to repaint the entire sky.

A colour match is made by mixing together as few colours as possible. The restorer will mix slightly more paint than he thinks will be required as it is difficult to mix exactly the same colour again if the paint is exhausted before retouching is completed.

The paint is built up in layers in the manner of the original painting. The restorer can imitate both colour and texture to near perfection but the spontaneity of the artist's strokes may never be matched, which is not as apparent in small retouchings as when large areas are involved.

The matching of colours is one of the most skilled operations in the restorer's repertoire, requiring a great deal of time and experience to perfect. Most old retouches have darkened with age, causing them to stand out as disfigurements rather than blend with the surrounding area. Contemporary retouches, unlike some of those of the past, are generally undetectable to the eye. Whether they will remain steadfast in years to come is open to speculation, although it is unlikely they will ever appear as discoloured as many earlier examples.

Several methods of matching colour and applying paint are used either individually or by combining different techniques such as glazing, scumbling, hatching, broken colour or stippling. Glazing, a favourite painting technique of the Old Masters, is invaluable for retouching. A glaze is a thin translucent colour layer, rich in medium, applied over opaque paint to increase luminosity.

THREE BASIC TECHNIQUES OF COLOUR MATCHING

1. One colour is painted over the area, which is then cross-hatched or stippled in a pointillistic manner with other colours to achieve an exact matching.
2. A lighter colour is painted over the area followed by glazing with

transparent colours until it has deepened to match the original paint. An attempt is made to imitate both the texture of the original paint and its present state of deterioration.

3. A darker colour is painted over the area, then a lighter partially opaque paint is scumbled on top. Variations in the thickness and texture of the scumbling are tried until correct matching is achieved.

The Technique of Retouching

Good light is essential for all retouching. An evenly distributed north light is preferred. Retouching is most difficult on a day when clouds intermittently obscure the sun. The variations of changing light can be frustrating when painstaking work is to be done. To overcome natural light variance, special fluorescent day lamps have been designed for retouching purposes. Although some restorers find them somewhat less ideal than natural light, there is much to be said for their constant unvarying illumination. Various magnification aids, such as the binocular magnifier attached by a headband, are invaluable for close work.

The dry pigment colours used by restorers are comparable in most respects to those used by artists. A new range of Cinquasia pigments of synthetic organic dyestuffs has been manufactured by Dupont. Tests show a superior light-fastness indicating that these pigments could supplant a number of colours in the violet and crimson range.

Most dry colour pigments suitable for restoring are available in good quality. Some colours which have been found useful for retouching purposes are titanium white, ivory black, burnt umber, raw umber, yellow ochre, Indian red, vermilion, cadmium yellow, cadmium red, viridian, terre verte, cobalt green, cobalt blue, ultramarine blue and Prussian blue.

The colours are mixed on a white palette or a sheet of glass over white paper. Deep dark colours are often the most difficult to imitate as they become increasingly transparent with time. Indian yellow is a useful pigment which may be glazed over deep blacks and browns without perceptibly lightening them.

A frequently used medium for retouching is egg tempera, which is suitable for retouching both oil and tempera paintings. The egg tempera medium is mixed by lightly beating a whole egg, placing it in a jar rinsed out with toluene and adding a few drops of distilled water. The synthetic resin MS2A crystals are dissolved in white spirit to be used for glazing.

The painting is carried out with fine quality sable brushes dipped in the medium and mixed with the pigments on the palette. The tempera is applied in successive semi-opaque layers and a glazing of wax and varnish or watercolour is added before the final picture varnish.

The advantage of tempera for retouching is that it may be used in a normal painting technique and colour matching is made comparatively easy. Tempera is quick-drying and durable. The disadvantage of tempera is that it becomes relatively insoluble with time.

As the need to remove the tempera may one day arise, an isolating layer of thin varnish is usually applied between the tempera coatings. The resin in the varnish can be easily softened by solvents, facilitating removal of the retouching if necessary.

The restorer adapts a style of retouching appropriate to the individual picture. The technique used for one picture may be quite unsuitable for another.

The consensus of opinion among restorers favours retouching to appear invisible, even to the point that if the original paint shows signs of abrasion or cracking, these will be imitated in the retouching. Retouches which are finished to blend invisibly should be recorded and photographed for reference.

RETOUCHING CRACKS

Cracks occurring in the paint layers or ground are usually indicative of age or stress. Age cracks and craquelure of a fine pattern are commonly associated with old paintings. Wide stress cracks, which are considered unsightly, may be retouched. If there are many cracks, retouching can become a time-consuming operation.

Cracks in dark areas of paint revealing a white ground can be alleviated by the application of a thin paint tint to the ground with a pointed brush.

Paint cracks or losses in a portrait are more disfiguring than those in a landscape painting. Although the cracks themselves may be the same size, they are more noticeable in a small painting than in a large one.

Revarnishing

The term revarnishing indicates that the old varnish has been removed from the picture and a new varnish coating applied.

It may be argued that pictures behind glass are better protected from inquisitive fingers, impurities in the atmosphere and the effects of un-filtered light sources than those that are varnished. Aesthetic considerations, however, make glass less desirable. The primary objection is the difficulty in viewing pictures because of distracting reflections. Glass alters colour tones and adds a further obscuring veil to darkening varnish.

Varnish serves as a protective layer against accidents, abrasions and unfavourable atmospheric conditions. A successful varnish coating must be hard enough to protect the painting and yet be easily removable in mild solvents. It should be resistant to bloom and cracking, and above all it should improve the appearance of the picture.

No single varnish has been found to be perfect. No substance easily removable, hard but flexible and non-yellowing, without injurious effect to the paint has yet been developed. The synthetic resin MS2A appears most closely to fulfill these exacting requirements. The synthetic resin Keytone N, which has replaced AW2, is a less expensive resin suitable for artists who wish to varnish their own pictures.

Polyvinyl acetate is highly esteemed as a surface coating by some restorers. The principal disadvantage of polyvinyl acetate is that rather strong solvents are required for its removal.

Preparing Varnish

Synthetic resin varnishes can be prepared in much the same manner as natural resins. A handful of resin crystals are placed in the toe of a silk stocking and immersed in a glass jar containing pure white spirit (BSS 245 specification). The purity of the white spirit is important as the lower grades of distillation are slow drying and prone to yellowing. Left overnight, the crystals will dissolve. The mixture can be thinned for spraying by the addition of more white spirit.

MATT VARNISH
It is sometimes desirable to reduce the light-reflecting gloss of varnish by adding a wax to obtain a matt effect. To prepare synthetic resin for matting, the resin dissolved in white spirit is poured into a double boiler, as it must not be heated over a direct flame. A piece of Cosmolloid synthetic wax (grade 80 hard) is melted over the mixture with an iron or spatula. A few drops added to the varnish are sufficient. The pan is placed in cold water and the mixture stirred until the wax has completely mixed.

VARNISH STORAGE
The clarity of varnish can be ascertained to a degree by placing the resin

with its proper solvent in a beaker and comparing the colour relationships. MS2A synthetic resin appears clear, dammar is yellow, mastic is a copper tone and copal is a dark brown.

Natural resin varnishes such as dammar or mastic form a brown sediment at the bottom of the container when left standing for long periods of time. Varnish appearing somewhat yellow in the jar will, when spread thinly on the picture surface, be clear even over light areas of paint.

Solvent solutions, such as white spirit or turpentine used for dissolving resins, should not be left stored in metal containers for long periods. Rust will begin to discolour the liquid contents and may adversely yellow the varnish. It is better to place the solvents in glass jugs or substantial polythene containers.

Applying Varnish by Spray

The varnishing of pictures should take place in a heated draught-free room. Application of the varnish is facilitated if the materials are allowed to warm to room temperature before use.

Most modern spray guns powered by air or electric compressors can be adjusted to spray a regulated mist of either a fine or a heavy consistency. Aerosol tins containing picture varnish are sold for spraying paintings; however, these allow for little density control.

It is preferable to spray the varnish rather than to apply it with a brush and risk damaging a fragile paint surface or lifting paint not completely dry. Paintings with wax-resin retouches are usually sprayed rather than brushed to ensure that the spirit contained in the varnish does not endanger the resin, which might otherwise be softened and shifted. Varnish may be either sprayed or brushed over most tempera or watercolour retouches, which are of a more stable nature.

Spraying may take place with the picture in an upright position provided the varnish is applied evenly. The consequence of an excess application is that the varnish will flow down the picture. The mist is sprayed back and forth across the picture with a constant motion and is carried beyond the edges of the painting. A subdued gloss may be obtained by holding the spray gun further from the picture. Additional layers may be added to increase the gloss after the first layer has dried. The spray should be directed at right-angles to the previous layer in order to reduce the possibility of streaks appearing in the varnish.

By spraying varnish, a uniform thickness can be built up gradually. A spray may be controlled to achieve less gloss than a solid-forming brush coating. Fine spray settles on the paint surface in small beads refracting light much like grains of sand. This is particularly advantageous for pictures on canvas, as the slight beading is harmonious with the canvas texture and reduces the glare caused by light on solid glossy varnish.

Occasionally certain oil colours used in painting tend to absorb more varnish than others, leaving dull patches on an otherwise glossy surface. These areas may be sprayed individually by reducing the air pressure of an adjustable spraygun and directing the mist in a circular motion.

Lacking a spray unit, varnish may be blown on with a mouth atomizer. A certain amount of lung power is required with this method and the varnish may be thinned to prevent the operator turning purple from exhaustion. It is best to lay the painting flat and spray the varnish in an arc up and over the painting to allow the mist to settle on the paint surface in a fine configuration.

Varnishing a picture with a compressor-operated spray gun

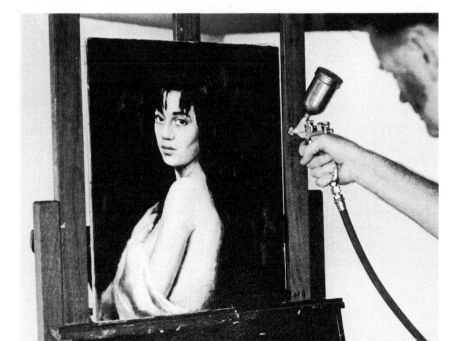

Applying Varnish by Brush

Varnish may be brushed on to pictures which have dry, stable paint surfaces that are free from dirt and flaking. A broad sable fan brush is useful. It is easily cleaned and the varnish flows from it with little pressure.

When the brush method of application is used, the picture is laid horizontally to allow the varnish to seek its own level. The varnish is brushed on in even overlapping strokes, beginning in the upper left corner and continuing across the picture. A second varnish coat may be added at right-angles to the first layer. Care must be taken to achieve a uniform blending of the varnish.

VARNISHING DAY

Most artists have observed the prescribed waiting period of twelve months to allow the paint to dry and harden before applying a final picture varnish, but some artists varnish their pictures before an exhibition in advance of the recommended period of time. Aware of the inherent danger in this practice, annual exhibition organizers, such as the Royal Academy, designate a 'Varnishing Day' preceding the private view. The artist is given a last-minute opportunity to retouch or varnish his paintings before the official opening of the exhibition. Contemporary artists may be seen carrying out this anachronism, sometimes with considerable showmanship, in full view of the attending press.

POLISHING WAX

Besides being incorporated into the varnish as a matting agent, wax may also be used to give an added lustre over varnish. A polishing wax for this purpose may be made from four parts Cosmolloid wax (80 hard) and one part grade 'A' wax melted together. The waxes are then poured into warm white spirit and stirred. The amount of white spirit should be sufficient to form the waxes into a consistency approximating that of a face cream. The prepared polishing wax may be stored in lidded jars.

The wax cream is rubbed over the varnished picture by hand, followed by buffing with a piece of silk. Wax applied by rubbing provides an excellent moisture barrier and is useful in reducing glare. If it becomes dirty, it may be removed with white spirit without damaging the underlying varnish. The wax coating should not be soft or dust and fluff will collect and become ingrained on the surface. Wax should not be used alone to protect the picture, as it is not tough enough.

CHAPTER X

FORGERY

Motivation

Forgery and imitation have existed since man first created objects admired and desired by others. Art forgeries flourished in ancient Greece and Rome. The exalted Michelangelo, in his youth, was persuaded by Lorenzo de Medici to give his sculptured statue of Cupid a patina of age in order to sell it fraudulently as an antique. This plot appealed to Michelangelo not so much for the financial gain but for the opportunity to match his skills with the early Greek sculptors. An added attraction in this deception was the prospect of fooling the art connoisseurs of the day.

Most copies and imitations of original works or those in the style of particular artists are done without fraudulent intent. A professor at an art school I once attended was walking along the corridor one day with what appeared to be a Renaissance painting under his arm. A student stopped him to admire the work and queried its age. We were astonished when he replied, 'Oh, I painted it about two weeks ago.' The professor was under contract to a nearby film studio and had been requested to produce an 'Old Master' to be used for a period film. His 'original' was painted in the accepted style and technique of an Old Master, complete with artificially induced craquelure and grime on a yellowed varnish. One wonders if this painting might one day be considered an attempt to defraud. It was certainly produced to deceive the eye, but fraud would exist only if an attempt were made to sell it as a genuine work of the period.

The forger is motivated by monetary prospects, an alter egoism in his talents and an overwhelming desire to deceive expert opinion. He is often an unsuccessful artist who, having failed in his attempts to become recognised, seeks his revenge on the art world. He derives immense satisfaction in the knowledge that his skills may one day embarrass the experts.

The public's imagination is captured by a Van Meegeren who succeeds in outwitting the critics and connoisseurs. Similarly the Great Train Robbery in Britain brought considerable universal admiration for its cunningly master-minded plan. Crimes executed with imagination and skill seem to outrage few. Years of imprisonment may be imposed for crimes of theft, yet art forgers are generally dealt with leniently. They seldom incur penalties of long prison sentences. Van Meegeren, whose career earned him considerable wealth, received a sentence of one year in prison while forgers of cheques and documents or counterfeiters of bank notes, coins or stamps are frequently given severe sentences. At times the courts seem to have judged the art forger as an impoverished artist who has succeeded merely in hoodwinking a small segment of society, namely the art collectors eager to acquire and the dealers anxious to profit.

Art forgers harbour an inner desire that the world should hear of their abilities and that learned art authorities and critics should be shown to be fallible. Most forgers who are exposed tell all; it may mark the end of their careers, but it is also their supreme moment of recognition. Many have found that forgery, like original creation, often leaves the artist small profit in comparison to the large sums of money received by the conspiring dealers. Disgruntled, he willingly exposes those involved in the swindle who, he feels, have reaped the rewards of his talent.

Art dealers, in addition to buying and selling pictures, advise and make assessments on behalf of clients. Their reputations are made by honest transactions. Occasionally, as in all fields, an unethical person infiltrates the profession and causes prejudicial publicity.

The Forger's Technique

The production of a forged painting is, in skilled hands, a technical achievement but little more. The attempt of a forger to emulate each stroke of the artist's brush is inconceivable, yet he can to some degree deceive the eye. In most instances the spurious painting lacks the spontaneity of the original. The faker, less inspired than the artist, achieves only a superficial imitation. Alongside the original, the copy appears emaciated, lacking the creative breath of artistic inspiration. Yet a few master forgers have managed to fool some of the experts.

The process of imitating an Old Master is laborious and time-consuming. The forger must be a painter of talent with a knowledge and interest in chemistry. In order to achieve success the aspiring forger will have read as much as possible about the artist and his methods of applying grounds, paints and glazes. He must be cognizant of recipes and materials that were in use at the time. Much of this research will require hours of intensive study of old manuscripts and treatises. Experiments involving chemical reactions, ageing and deterioration must be undertaken.

Having decided to paint a fake characteristic of a particular Old Master, the forger searches to find an unimportant painting of the same period which may be bought cheaply. A commercial paint remover is used to strip away the old varnish and layers of paint, and a new ground is applied to the canvas.

The colours used must be similar to those of the artist who is being forged. The correct substances must be obtained to grind into pigment with the appropriate oils. White lead was used by the Old Masters and is of paramount importance. It shields the paint layers from X-rays used for detection and it is susceptible to cracking, which is induced to give the painting an appropriate look of age. The most difficult and expensive colour to obtain is genuine ultramarine (lapis lazuli). It was used by many of the Old Masters to paint robes and drapery.

The painting is executed in a manner characteristic of the particular Old Master. Hardening agents can be used to make the paint film impervious to tests of solubility, which might be carried out in an examination. The increasing number of plastic derivatives may afford the forger unexplored areas of simulating the toughness of centuries-old oil paint.

Forgers have employed ovens to aid in the drying and hardening of the oil paint. The canvas is removed carefully from the stretcher and prepared for the induced ageing procedure. The natural process of evaporation and hardening of the paint layers may require fifty years or longer, but by the use of the oven the appearance of two centuries of drying may be achieved in a day.

Cracks caused by time and stress usually penetrate deeply through the paint layers to the priming. False cracks drawn with a needle leave characteristically smooth edges and go only as deep as the paint layers. Cracks have been artificially induced by rolling the painting over a cylinder several times or by pressing the canvas from the back with the fingers. Dirt is rubbed into the cracks and the canvas put back on the original stretchers. The methods used are often rather crude. If subjected to microscopic examination the artificially induced cracks in the paint layers show an identifiable variation when compared with natural cleavage caused by age and stress. One method of circumventing this identification is carefully to scrape an old painting with natural deep cracks to the ground. When it is overpainted and baked, the original cracks in the ground will reappear in the new paint. Varnish applied over the baked paint surface assumes a similar crackle pattern.

Apparent damage is often inflicted on the fake to create an aura of authenticity and age. Flaking of the paint may be induced, deliberate scratches made or areas of the picture sanded to indicate abrasive wear and the passage of time. To further the subterfuge, some of these areas may be retouched to suggest that the painting had been previously restored. Such retouchings are not done too skilfully or they may pass unnoticed.

SIGNATURES

A great many forgeries have involved nothing more than the alteration of the signature by either overpainting or scraping the original. An unsigned work of a minor painter of the period may pass for the work of a more important master by the addition of his forged signature. Many vendors with little skill in art have become accomplished forgers of signatures. They obliterate and change artist's names on paintings of similar schools. The false signature is often indistinguishable from the original. Tampering can be detected with the aid of the microscope and infra-red photography.

Most old paintings are covered by a network of fine cracks which also appear in the paint the artist used for his signature. If a false signature is added at a much later date, the microscope will show it lacks a similar craquelure. Some forgers scrape away varnish and paint to forge the signature and create an impression that it is located in depth as an integral part of the paint layer. Infra-red rays and X-rays can expose marks caused by scraping.

ARRANGING THE 'DISCOVERY'

The forger will take pains to assure that apparently natural circumstances surround the finding of his painting. By so doing he will hope to eliminate any suspicions that may lead to close scientific investigation. He is audacious enough to believe his skill will fool the experts conducting a visual examination of the painting.

Most 'discoveries' have been the result of a conspiracy between the forger, an unscrupulous dealer and sometimes a third party. Claims that paintings have been found in attics of old houses or stored away by an eccentric great-grandfather are among the ruses used. Most fraudulent paintings appear on the market with equally fraudulent historical backgrounds. Supporting documents of alleged authenticity, bills of sale, letters from the artist and dealers describing the work are as frequently forged as the suspect works themselves. In addition, phony auction sales notices and catalogues listing the painting in important collections are a common means of assuring the prospective client of the painting's authenticity.

An ingenious technique employed by a few forgers is to paint a nondescript picture over the fake. The picture is taken to a restorer on the pretext of having it cleaned. The restorer recognises that it has obviously been overpainted and recommends its removal in all good faith. The client readily agrees. The restorer carefully strips the overpaint, revealing a possibly important painting underneath. The client is informed of the find and agrees to have the picture examined by an art authority — preferably one who has not yet achieved great distinction in his field.

AUTHENTICATION

The art authority is greatly influenced by a seemingly accidental discovery made in the studio of a reputable restorer. He is at all times anxious to separate the genuine from the spurious. He will probably have spent countless hours examining sometimes genuine but usually unimportant paintings brought to his attention by owners in the hope of monetary gain — then here at last is a work in the style of a known painter revealed in a credible manner. The painting is admittedly not a masterpiece but is important nevertheless. The innocent expert all too willingly plays his part in the drama. His natural scepticism gives way to the skill of the forger, the report of the restorer and the client's convincing story of his having bought the painting in an old junk shop. The press is called in and with his authentication the painting enters the art sales market with its alleged value considerably increased by publicity.

The expert may pause to reflect on some niggling doubt about the picture, but by this stage he is a committed man. A parallel to this may be found in the perpetrated hoax of the 'Piltdown Man' whose alleged skull for many years divided anthropological opinion. Many wrongful attributions have been left undisclosed in fear of mockery. The fear of being found wrong is not confined to art historians. When the judges of an art exhibition were faced with the news that a picture they had just awarded first prize was, in fact, painted by a chimpanzee, they allowed that he was 'a particularly gifted ape' and that the work was of sufficient merit for the award.

ATTRIBUTIONS

The art scholar proven wrong in his conclusions is much maligned by those, who in their ignorance, find solace in thinking that the experts are really no more knowledgeable than themselves. Little publicity is given when they correctly recognize wrongly attributed works. An example is 'The Music Lesson' in the British Royal Collection. This valuable Vermeer had been purchased by George III in 1762 as a work by a minor painter named Frans van Mieris. Few experts today venture a written opinion of an important picture without first evaluating the results of a laboratory examination.

Assigning attributions becomes exceedingly difficult when several artists may have had their hand in the painting of a picture. Rubens employed a number of painters to assist him in filling the numerous commissions he was given. Among these assistants was Anthony van Dyck, whose work is often identifiable. The assistants were generally specialists in painting landscapes, backgrounds, robes or still life included in the composition. The master normally painted the central figures and particularly the exposed flesh, although even these were often underpainted by another artist.

The historian is able to use his knowledge of the period, dress, literary references and other factors in making his attribution. Some fakes have been revealed by the forger's lack of historical knowledge. In attempting to create an unknown work that a particular master might have painted, he may stumble by including a costume or a piece of furniture of later date than would have existed in a genuine painting of the period.

Unattributed paintings in the hands of a dealer soon become white elephants. The dealer may try to persuade certain acknowledged experts that the picture is by a known painter. Such requests have even been accompanied by offers of remuneration. Few experts are likely to risk their reputations in this way.

AUCTIONEERS AND DEALERS

Many books on forgery have included a variation of the quotation, 'Corot painted 2,000 pictures in his life, of which 3,000 are in America.' As this statement indicates, buying a painting is somewhat of a gamble.

I have attended minor auction sales where paintings variously described as by 'Constable' and by 'Gainsborough' were sold for piddling sums amidst good-natured guffaws by the assembly. They were signed on the canvas and presented in Barbizon frames with engraved brass name-plates.

Relatively few paintings on the market are accompanied by documentation as to their authenticity. Reputable auction salesrooms are keenly aware of the need for correct identification of works assigned to them for auction. One of the most respected firms, Sotheby, in London, has a catalogue coding system that the potential buyer may readily decipher. In 1959 Sotheby published a catalogue with the following notice:

NOTICE APPLICABLE TO SALES OF OLD MASTER AND 18TH/19TH CENTURY
PAINTINGS AND DRAWINGS

Sotheby & Co. for themselves and for the seller of each Lot give notice to intending Purchasers that in accordance with longstanding practice in Fine Art Sale Rooms in London, certain terms used in descriptions of Lots contained in Sotheby & Co.'s catalogues have by convention the meanings ascribed to them in the Glossary below:
Glossary:

The christian name(s) and surname of the artist:
In our opinion a work by the artist.

The initials of the christian name(s) and the surname of the artist:
In our opinion a work of the period of the artist which may be wholly or in part his work.

The surname only of the artist:
In our opinion a work of the school or by one of the followers of the artist or in his style.

'After' followed by the surname of the artist:
In our opinion a copy of the work of the artist.

'Signed':
Has a signature which in our opinion is the signature of the artist.

'Bears signature' or 'Inscribed (with the artist's name)':
Has a signature which in our opinion may be the signature of the artist.

'Dated':
Is so dated and in our opinion was executed at that date.

'Bears date' or 'Inscribed (with date)':
Is so dated and in our opinion may have been executed at about that date.

Sotheby & Co.

The most renowned dealers have unwittingly acquired and sold faked paintings to clients. Should the vendor be unaware of a painting's origin, it could be said to have been sold in good faith, whereupon a full refund would be in order. Dealers of repute are prepared to buy back any work

subsequently found to be suspect. Integrity is a hallmark closely guarded
in the art world. At the merest hint of scandal, reputable dealers will
sustain losses in order to protect their good names. In several cases the
police have been aware that dealers of impeccable reputation had been
hoodwinked into purchasing the works of clever forgers. A dealer may
refuse to prosecute or even admit the purchase had been made, because
publicity naming him as the dupe of a swindle is most undesirable. Dealers
are not infallible. Many paintings with seemingly genuine documentation
have started life as fakes, perpetuated by inclusion in well-known
collections.

Scientific Detection and the Expert

The scientific examination of a painting by a highly qualified restorer
offers the most conclusive proof that it is genuine. The art historian's
opinion is substantiated by the restorer's findings. Science can prove or
disprove that a painting is consistent in its supposed date of execution, and
the use of materials available at the time. X-rays can reveal if there is
another painting underneath. The results of scientific analysis are
presented for the historian to interpret in many instances. In the past,
judgments were primarily based on style and brushwork with a few rather
rudimentary chemical tests given to paints and varnishes. Today a full
range of scientific studies may be employed to aid the expert in making a
complete evaluation.

The scientific analysis of painting materials, conducted with the same
thoroughness of the forensic scientist, has sharply curtailed the modern
forger's confidence in attempting any grand scale forgeries of antiquities.
The increased use of X-rays, microphotography, pigment analysis and
other modern investigatory equipment designed for the examination of
paintings would not permit a forger like Van Meegeren to succeed today.
Masterful forgeries might still be undetected by the connoisseur and even
the art historian without scientific aids. The gifted craftsman/forger can
develop an uncanny flair for imitating the most deft strokes and flourishes
of the artist. This is especially true in the case of Van Meegeren, who did
not attempt to forge existing Vermeers, but created works similar in style
to his early paintings.

The use of X-rays and infra-red photographs have been a great asset to
the historian in determining the authenticity of paintings. Comparison
between an original Rembrandt painting and a copy will reveal the slow,

studied and indirect manner of the copyist as opposed to the quick, decisive and inspired brush of Rembrandt. In the case of paintings on wood, X-rays may show the later addition of a missing panel section. Radiographs have revealed artificially induced wormholes drilled straight into panels unlike the natural irregular direction taken by a burrowing pest. Even nails can be identified as to their approximate date of manufacture. Many fake panel pictures, supposedly painted before the eighteenth century, have been exposed by the detection of wire nails which were not invented until sometime later.

Radiographs and infra-red photographs provide useful information about the individual mannerisms and the way the artist builds up a picture. The photographs can reveal the actual stages of a painting's development from preliminary sketching to the final decisive paint strokes. Scientific examination may show that the painting is of the presumed date, but it is left to the historian ultimately to determine if it is the genuine work of an individual master or a skilful copy executed at the time. Perhaps forgers in the future may use radiographs and infra-red photographs to improve their techniques.

The various types of equipment used in the restorer's laboratory are more fully described in Chapter VI on Examination.

A REMBRANDT FORGERY

The ingenuity of the forger and his accomplices is sometimes remarkable. A case related by Sepp Schuller in his book *Forgers, Dealers, Experts* is an example. A Florentine art dealer had a copy made of a painting by Rembrandt of his son Titus. The copy was painted on canvas of the proper period, Rembrandt's forged signature was overpainted with tempera and an imaginary signature added with the words 'Copy after Rembrandt'. The work was then shipped to a conspiring American dealer in New York. While en route, the US Customs authorities were informed that a Florentine dealer, using an assumed name, was trying to avoid duty on a genuine Rembrandt by having the artist's signature overpainted and labelled a copy. When the American dealer called for the package, customs officials told him it was an attempt by the Italian dealer to smuggle a genuine Rembrandt. The American dealer appeared incredulous, but he was finally 'convinced' when the faintly visible outline of Rembrandt's signature was pointed out. Feigning reluctance, he paid the fine and the duty. The result of this cunningly contrived deception was convincing proof, furnished by the customs authorities, that the picture was indeed a genuine

Rembrandt. The subsequent sale of the painting resulted in a profit far exceeding the fine and duty imposed.

Van Meegeren, Master Forger

In the light of the multitude of articles and books about the extraordinary forging career of Hans Van Meegeren, it seems superfluous to repeat the story. A brief recounting of the highlights together with a few fresh observations seems necessary.

In 1961 a stage play was produced in London entitled *Masterpiece* which told the Van Meegeren story, and Lord Kilbracken's book *Van Meegeren* gives a detailed account of his life and forging techniques.

Van Meegeren worked as an artist in his native Holland, creating insignificant paintings which were on occasion used for commercial reproduction. His personal vision was banal and uninspired. Reacting to the scorn of art critics to his work, he set about preparing in the 1930s for his ultimate revenge and vindication as the artist of genius he considered himself to be. Van Meegeren studied and experimented with the materials and techniques of the Old Masters. He forged and sold the works of many painters besides the well-known Vermeers. Acting as his own agent, he shared neither the secret nor the profit. His undoing came about after World War II when he was brought to trial in 1947 for having sold a 'national treasure', a Vermeer painting, to one of the Nazi chiefs, Hermann Goering. While in prison, he painted another Vermeer to prove to disbelieving authorities that he was not a traitor but the most successful forger of all time. The total profits of his forgery sales amounted to over £700,000 ($1,680,000), an amount that would be equivalent to nearly treble that figure today.

The war provided a convenient cover for his activities. Had any of his pictures been subjected to laboratory analysis they would have been discovered, for even at that time scientific examination was sufficiently advanced. The war also created a problem for him in that his source of the important pigment lapis lazuli was closed. During his trial the results of the scientific examination by the expert Dr Paul Coremans confirmed the use of cobalt blue, a colour unknown in Vermeer's time.

Van Meegeren's greatest work, 'Christ at Emmaus', was sold to the Rembrandt Society in 1937. He chose a religious painting as there is only one known work by Vermeer of this subject. Armed with the information that as a youth Vermeer was influenced by the Italian artist Caravaggio, he created a work in the style Vermeer might have employed at that time. Van Meegeren explained to interrogators that he had painted it over a canvas on which had been previously painted the head of a child. Ultimately a radiograph proved his contention. Following the trial, 'Christ at Emmaus' was relegated in disgrace to languish in the vaults of the Rotterdam museum, its value reduced to nil. One wonders what price it might fetch on the market today if offered for sale. Its value has certainly risen considerably as an historical curiosity if not as a work of art. Perhaps one day we may see artists forging Van Meegeren forgeries.

'The Procuress', a work Van Meegeren copied about the year 1940 after the seventeenth-century Dutch painter Dirck van Baburen, now hangs in the Courtauld Institute, London. This is the only forgery by Van Meegeren in England — it is hoped!

Copies

Copies of paintings have been made by art students for their own instruction which unscrupulous persons have later attempted to pass off as genuine works. In earlier times students were encouraged to copy their master's work, frequently with the master adding touches himself. To further confuse expert opinion, some copies of paintings have been signed by the masters themselves. Corot and Utrillo in particular signed the works of pupils which they considered to be of merit. Many of the great architects have signed architectural plans conceived and drawn by lesser-known architects in their employ.

Peter Paul Rubens (1577-1640) employed many artists and assistants with whom he collaborated on paintings. Prominent amongst them was the subsequently celebrated artist Anthony van Dyck (1599-1641). In a letter to an English collector, Sir Dudley Carlton, Rubens wrote quite candidly regarding a copy of his own work by a pupil. This was noted by Sepp Schuller in his book *Forgers, Dealers, Experts*. Rubens wrote, 'As this reproduction is not yet quite completed I am going to retouch it throughout myself, so that it can pass for an original if necessary.' He further wrote in regard to other copies, 'I have retouched them to such effect that they can hardly be distinguished from the originals . . . they are perfect miracles at the price.'

Drawings and paintings are often created as preliminary studies. These are generally loosely sketched and provide the artist with a guide for future compositions. One well-known British artist is reputed to produce 'preliminary studies' in drawing and gouache of his own pictures many years after the paintings have been completed.

Honestly made copies can be turned into forgeries by the addition of signatures, initials or monograms. Unknown names have been removed from paintings and prints and famous ones added in order to sell them as originals. Dates have been added or existing dates altered with a single paint stroke. Copies can prove valuable; had it not been for Battista Franco's copy of Michelangelo's 'Noli Mi Tangere' we would have no record of the painting. The copy exists as the only evidence of the destroyed original.

Duplicates or copies have been made of their own works by many painters. El Greco, for instance, was requested to paint three complete sets of his portraits of Christ's Disciples. In the days of the great artist's studios, such commissions were common and desirable. They helped to keep the artists' assistants and apprentices continuously employed.

In modern times there has been a feeling that the artist is compromising his integrity by copying his own work. Popular pictures offer a temptation for artists to make duplicates. How many times have I heard at private views, 'That is a fine picture, I would like to buy it but I see it has been sold' — a fairly safe statement for the gallery visitor to make. What a surprise would be in store if the artist could reply, 'I have another copy in the back room — excuse me while I fetch it.' A few contemporary artists do take commissions to paint replicas of their own works. Unless these are documented, there will be no way of determining which paintings are the originals.

Reproductions

Artists may be seen copying paintings in most important public museums and art galleries. Many of the copyists are students, others are professional artists commissioned to reproduce works for clients. Might not these be future forgery prospects? Certainly this is borne in mind by most institutions, who require artists' copies of works in their collection to be either slightly smaller or larger than the original.

While individual copies are painstakingly painted by artists in museums, modern photographic reproductions are being printed by the thousands on surfaces simulating the raised paint layers and brush strokes of the original. One technique utilizes photographic reproductions laid on to board or canvas and overpainted with layers of genuine oil colours by teams of artists using assembly line techniques. Another deceptive method is a reproduction on paper of an old painting, fixed and ironed on to a wooden panel. False fissures and wormholes are added to create the appearance of age. The cracks in the reproduction are incised with tools and the picture discoloured, after which an artificially yellowed varnish is applied in thick layers. The finished product is remarkably realistic.

Photographs of original paintings can be transferred to a photo-sensitised canvas for overpainting. Another useful aid for the copyist is a balopticon, a form of projecting lantern, permitting the projection of a postcard reproduction on to a canvas. This may be enlarged to the actual dimensions of the original painting, then traced and painted.

GRAPHICS

The art market is saturated with falsely issued prints which have been intentionally forged or copied. The client must rely on the expertise of a reputable dealer to ensure that a work is genuine. If a print passes his scrutiny the client can feel secure that should any subsequent discovery indicate that the print is not genuine, the dealer will buy it back and sustain the loss.

There are countless stories to illustrate the forger's ingenuity in placing prints on the market. A collection of Corot figure drawings in various media, reported to have come from the artist's studio, were brought to light by a Doctor Jousseaumet of Paris. They were accepted as genuine by distinguished experts and in 1928 they found their way into a number of public and private collections. To add to the appearance of authenticity some rather intimate and even indecent inscriptions were written on some of them. These drawings are all now discredited.

Prints and drawings have been cunningly altered and missing portions added in pencil, chalk or ink. Artists' and collectors' marks and stamps, such as Whistler's famous butterfly monogram, were readily forged. The graphic expert is continually challenged by such forgeries. To add to his difficulties many artists encouraged their pupils to make precise copies of their work. The expert has a decided advantage in the detection of spurious works if he can obtain an authentic original for comparison. Unlike a painting, print originals are multiple. Variations of line and tone can be compared and the paper tested to determine if it is of the correct age and method of manufacture.

Prints often provided a means of artistic communication in the days when travel was long and arduous. Italian and Flemish artists were influenced by each other's prints and sometimes used them as inspiration or copied them as paintings. The deliberate copying of Albrecht Dürer's engravings and woodcuts was so proliferate that an imitator was taken to the magistrate by Dürer's widow. She was eventually forced to buy the spurious blocks to prevent further prints from being issued. In more recent times coloured Japanese prints were highly esteemed by the Impressionists, who were greatly influenced by them.

Although it is not technically a forgery, the practice of cutting pictures into fragments to realize greater profit is certainly a deception. A Cézanne still life painting depicting apples was cut into separate compositions and sold individually by a Paris dealer. Mutilations of this nature are not confined to paintings. Original prints are removed from bound volumes to be sold at a handsome profit. Books on the subject of etching may contain valuable original prints taken directly from plates by such artists as Rembrandt and Whistler. Etching plates are able to withstand the large editions pulled for book publishing by having a thin steel facing applied over their surface. Some editions included excellent heliogravure reproductions, which are frequently passed off as originals. Complete books containing reproductions of paintings and maps are dissected and sold as separate pages. The profit realized by these sales can amount to several times the price of the bound books.

Etchings and lithographs pulled by the artist or a professional printer and approved by the artist are considered original works. Yet those pulled at a later date by unauthorized persons are still considered original but reduced in value because of the circumstances involved. Prints signed in pencil or ink on the paper and not in the plate generally bring higher prices. This gives evidence that the artist himself approved the work. A great number of prints in existence today were not printed under the artist's supervision. Prints have been issued from surviving original plates that have been in the hands of museums, publishers, dealers and art speculators for generations. Until a few years ago, prints taken from original Rembrandt plates in the possession of a museum were offered for nominal sums to professional artists and students. I have seen a J. M. Whistler etching plate being inked and prints taken at an art school. The paper used contained a watermark of the correct year and manufacture. All of these occurrences make the final determination of a print's originality and value a matter for the expert.

The continued inking, wiping and pressure exerted by the press rollers reduce the quality of successive prints. Therefore early impressions are generally richer, more contrasting and consequently more sought after. As the metal wears, subsequent prints become lack-lustre. Blacks are reduced to greys and etched lines become faint. Unscrupulous persons have attempted to rework these plates in order to infiltrate the art market with fraudulent early impressions. Another abhorrent practice is the sale of etchings from plates which have been cancelled. Cancellation is accomplished by incised lines drawn across the plate or holes drilled through it. This mutilation inflicted by the artist serves to indicate the end of the edition and the artist's wish that no further prints should be pulled.

The French artist Jacques Villon achieved his own late fame after spending many years copying and making etchings of designs by Braque and Picasso. Upon viewing and correcting the proofs, these artists approved the printing of limited editions which they subsequently signed. Many engravings and lithographs of the eighteenth and nineteenth centuries were more candidly presented. They printed the names of artists, engravers, printers and publishers. A good many black and white prints from this period have been overpainted with oils or watercolours and transformed into highly coloured pictures. This was common practice with engravings by certain masters and later became widespread with topographic and sporting prints.

Reproductions of lithographs by Miro, Leger and Picasso have been torn from magazines and sold as originals. Current reproductions of a popular British watercolour painter are faithfully printed on heavy watercolour paper. Some of these are signed and numbered by the artist. Collectors might be misled into thinking they are originals.

A complete essay on the ethics of making and selling prints is contained in an inexpensive, concise publication *What is an Original Print?* which was published by the Print Council of America and is available in Britain.

STAMPS

A lucrative international trade exists in forged rare stamps. As prices rise on the market, forgery in this field is rapidly increasing.

An interesting development is the emergence of a small group of highly skilled experts who specialize in stamp restoration. The stamp forger uses specialized equipment in his work. Improving the condition of stamps is one thing but alterations to increase their value to collectors is another. It might be argued that restorers in every field are doing much the same thing — increasing the value of a work through cleaning and alteration.

In the art world, restoration is considered the improvement by preservation of a work created by an individual. Alterations are viewed as unethical, but only an attempt to offer known forgeries for sale is fraudulent and liable to prosecution.

The law takes a dim view of some of the practices of stamp forgers, perhaps because the stamps are issued by governments and therefore come under similar restrictions as minted currency.

The British Museum Exhibition

One of the most popular exhibitions to have been staged by the British Museum Printroom in recent years was the 1963 exhibition entitled 'Forgeries and Deceptive Copies'. Included in the exhibition were art forgeries of Rembrandt, Watteau, Turner, Raphael and Hogarth. Besides drawing, print and painting forgeries, the exhibition displayed manuscripts, books, antiquities, natural history specimens, postage stamps, coins and medals. Wherever possible, genuine and false specimens were shown side by side. Several museums were persuaded to divulge their locked storeroom secrets. The assembling of the exhibition required delicate persuasion. Few museum directors are proud of acquiring a bogus work of art. The normally sedate British Museum was turned into a kind of Rogues' Gallery where one might with impunity shout, 'Fake'.

The exhibition included examples of not only the master forgers but also the cruder attempts of the inept. One Italian forger who copied many of Hogarth's prints did so with pen and watercolour on Italian paper. Some unenlightened forgers have signed false signatures of artists who are known to have never, or rarely ever, signed their work.

A nineteenth-century carpenter and builder named Peter Thompson created a mythical artist, 'Captain John Eyre', who was supposed to have been born in England in 1604. Thompson published a distinguished biography and ancestral lineage for the Captain stating that he had served under Cromwell. He showed numerous excellent pen drawings of London scenes, purported to have been drawn by the artist. They were embellished with quaint old English script, using such delightful phrases as 'In ye next week to do master Shakespeare's house in ye clink streete.' Antiquarians were unable to resist this charming touch and sales followed. Thompson later circulated a suite of etchings under the guise of Captain Eyre. A list of subscribers headed by the Prince Consort was prepared. Fortunately some doubt was raised about the authenticity of the work before the Royal Family were involved as innocent dupes, and Thompson was unmasked as having been the artist. Many of his works are still in circulation with erroneous attributions and dated as having been executed in the seventeenth century.

Among the exhibits of fakes was a very fine statue entitled 'Flora' supposedly by Leonardo da Vinci. A picture of a nude woman holding a bunch of flowers painted in the manner of Leonardo led to this novel forgery. In the 1840s a dealer named Buchanan engaged the Victorian sculptor, Richard Cockle Lucas, to model a life-size bust in wax after the painting. It was given the name of 'Flora'. In 1904 the statue was sold at auction along with his effects. Subsequently the wax bust came into the London art market as being attributed to Leonardo. In 1909 it was acquired by Mr Murray Marks, who sold it for the sum of eight thousand pounds to the Kaiser Friedrich Museum, Berlin, as a genuine Leonardo da Vinci. He had previously offered it to the British Museum, who wisely declined to purchase it. The eminent director Dr Wilhelm van Bode's reputation suffered as a result of the purchase. The matter was blown out of all proportion when he declined to admit his error.

It is an uncomfortable thought that the British Museum exhibition displayed only the unmasked frauds. How many more fraudulent works remain in public collections?

Modern Paintings

Since World War II collectors who buy works of art for speculative investment have found few important Old Master and Impressionist paintings for sale as most of them are now in museum collections. The collectors have turned to modern 'name' painters as a better investment than stocks and bonds. With the current demand for the Modern Masters, many forgers today apply their talents to imitating fashionable modern works that are almost as lucrative. The time required to knock out a passable Picasso does not compare with the technical involvement of a Vermeer forgery. A modern work requires only imitation of style and the easily acquired contemporary materials used by the artist. There is no need to create a veneer of great age. Scientific examination and analysis have made the forgery of Old Master paintings dangerous and unrewarding for the prospective forger. False documents and other references of authenticity may still be required but even these are unnecessary as long as the picture 'looks right'.

A factor advantageous to the forger is the large number of works produced by many Modern Masters. The artist himself is sometimes unable to identify a particular work as being by his own hand when presented with a really clever facsimile. A curious example of this occurred when the Italian metaphysical artist Giorgio de Chirico became a persona non grata with galleries exhibiting his early works in collections. He insisted on denouncing paintings as fakes which were proved beyond doubt to be by his hand. Apparently he disapproved of these works if they did not meet his standards after the intervening years. Many artists share this feeling upon seeing their early work again after a lengthy interval.

A few years ago a Swiss art gallery owner set out to create an unknown artist. He believed that simply through the use of his publicity and gallery connections he could promote any minor artist to the ranks of a Modern Master. The paintings he showed were in the modern idiom and soon the artist was being exhibited in several prominent galleries on the Continent and scheduled for a New York exhibition. He was described as an artist of mid-European origins in articles praising his composition and style. The hoax was revealed by the dealer when he finally admitted to an inquiring art journalist that he was the artist and had painted the pictures himself. Not to be outdone, the critics wrote that in spite of their unorthodox presentation, the works were of a very high standard. This perhaps indicated that the dealer's original contention is of some merit.

A SWINDLE IN LONDON

The forging of modern works has a particular appeal for a few young artists who have not achieved recognition through their own pictures. Though many young artists fail in their bid for success, few have the particular talents required to become master forgers. It seems worth relating the story of one who did and the notoriety he attracted.

During 1961 Jean Pierre Schecroun, an artist already accomplished in forgery, made a journey to London with his painting equipment and two assistants. The assistants laid the groundwork for the conspiracy by visiting the Mayfair galleries posing as important dealers from Paris. They gathered information through enquiries about the particular Modern Masters each gallery was interested in acquiring. Following his accomplices' reports Schecroun sat in his hotel room and painted to order a 'Leger' for this gallery, a 'Pollock' for another. In less than two weeks the team disposed of thirty pictures for £20,000 ($48,000). They returned to Paris elated with their successful expedition. This elation was short lived. Two London dealers happened to get together and showed each other their new acquisitions. They were highly chagrined when they discovered that the water-colours of 'Soulages' and the work of 'Braque' were painted on the same type of paper. A quick check with the Galerie Maeght in Paris confirmed the forgery.

In Paris in 1963 Schecroun and his accomplices were convicted of the forgery of seventy-nine works. Schecroun was given a four-year suspended sentence and fined the equivalent of about £1,000 ($2,400). The accused were ordered to pay approximately £10,000 ($24,000) damages to the plagiarized artists and the swindled purchasers. After being sentenced Schecroun said he would devote himself to preparing for exhibitions of his own work.

THE DAVID STEIN CAPER

An interesting case of modern forgery was related on BBC television in November, 1969. It concerned David Stein, a young half-British, half-French artist, who in 1962 met a French forger who showed Stein his fakes of Picasso and Miro hanging on the walls of his Paris apartment. Greatly impressed, Stein thought his own talents could be put to similar use. So began the brief but rewarding career of another clever forger. Stein's first attempt at faking and selling a Picasso met with instant success. He continued to improve his technique and his repertoire of Modern Masters grew. He did not attempt to copy slavishly but he created new compositions characteristically incorporating elements of the master's work into his painting. Stein likes to call them 'original Fakes'.

Stein copied only the works of artists he admired. He explains his working life as a kind of Jekyll and Hyde existence. 'You become someone else when you are painting. When I paint Matisse, I become Matisse. When I paint Chagall, I am Chagall.' He claims to identify himself with the mind and the soul of the artist he is imitating. Most successful forgers have done this to some degree.

In 1964 Stein met and married Anne Marie. An expensive honeymoon was paid for by the proceeds of the sale of a faked Picasso. Anne Marie aided and abetted Stein to the extent of learning to apply tea stains to paper in order to give it the appearance of age.

The Steins opened a New York gallery in Park Avenue in 1965. They originally intended to sell only genuine paintings but as Stein explained, 'I started painting these Chagalls and Picassos mostly because I wanted to improve the business when I was under financial pressure. My goal was to sell legitimate paintings.' Another gallery was opened in Palm Beach,

Florida. They lived expensively, employing servants and a chauffeur for their Rolls-Royce.

Stein's ultimate undoing came about through his almost miraculous ability to provide Chagalls for the many clients who requested them. In one morning he painted three Chagall watercolours to effect a sale he was arranging with another dealer. By afternoon the deal had been completed and Stein was richer by more than four thousand pounds. The paintings were signed and accompanied by certificates of authenticity. His nefarious activities finally came to the attention of the Art Association of America, whose membership includes some seventy leading art dealers. A memorandum containing a description of David Stein was sent to the members. Irving Young, a dealer who had purchased some of the fake Chagalls, complained to the New York District Attorney's Office. Assistant District Attorney Joseph Stone took the suspect Chagall watercolours to Mr Marc Chagall who was in New York to unveil the murals he had created for the Metropolitan Opera House. Stone said that when he showed the paintings to Chagall, 'He became furious. He told me that these were not his work, that they were certainly poor reproductions or poor pastiches and that he wanted very much to destroy them. As a matter of fact he was on the verge of actually tearing one of them when I asked him to please desist and explained to him that we had just commenced an investigation, that there were probably other works of his that had been counterfeited and that we would appreciate his cooperation in his not destroying the painting and in cooperating with this office.'

The Steins fled to California after narrowly escaping arrest by the New York Police. He was soon apprehended and, while awaiting trial, he continued to produce fraudulent Picasso drawings and Chagall watercolours. He was eventually sentenced to an eight-month term of imprisonment.

Stein now claims to be finished with forgery. Ever confident of his abilities as a forger, he has set his sights on becoming an artist in his own right. He says, 'Instead of using other artists' names, I want to use mine. I have already started. I have people who are very interested in opening a gallery for me. I am very confident I can accomplish myself in art.'

He seems to have succeeded. A London art gallery staged a much publicized exhibition of his work. Prices ranged from fifty to two hundred pounds, quite modest in comparison to the prices he commanded in his role as a forger/dealer.

Who knows if the temptation for the modern forger can really be discouraged when there is an insatiable market demanding the work of name artists? Perhaps in this age of enlightenment in which associations are formed for group therapy to resist alcohol and gambling, a club might be inaugurated for the rehabilitation of art forgers.

The number of fakes exchanging hands raises the question in every collector's mind about every painting — Is it genuine? The only absolute guarantee of authenticity for the collector/investor is to buy the work of a talented but as yet undiscovered artist. Not only would the amount of money invested be small, but the purchase would benefit a living artist. It is better not to wait; within a year of the French artist Bernard Buffet becoming a celebrated artist, forgeries of his sparse style appeared in several parts of the world.

CHAPTER XI

THE FLORENCE FLOOD

The patients lay in a long corridor on their hastily erected steel bunk beds. They were soaked and besmirched with mud and oil. The scene was one of despair. Volunteers, anguish etched on their faces, tenderly carried in new patients. Would the patients survive the catastrophe? Who could save them?

These patients were beyond the help of any medical doctor. They were not human patients in a hospital, but Renaissance paintings, the heritage of the art world, being stored in a humidity controlled environment. In this atmosphere, these masterpieces in peril awaited rescue by restorers from many nations. The Florence flood of 1966 was to focus the world's attention on the restoring profession, whose dedicated skills and technical achievements had remained unacclaimed.

Deluge

Just before dawn on 4 November 1966, following days of torrential rain, the River Arno burst its banks, inundating the countryside and the still sleeping city of Florence. The citadel of Renaissance art treasures and history was endangered along with the lives of her inhabitants. The flood caught the city unprotected and vulnerable, her citizens asleep in their beds.

The rampaging floodwaters swept through the streets at a speed of thirty-six miles per hour, carrying everything before it. The night was filled with terrifying noises. Trees and cars were lifted like matchsticks and toys to cascade and scrape against buildings like dodge-'em cars at a fair. Flotsam of all descriptions was swept along, junk mingling with jewels. Into these cataracts spilled great quantities of black fuel oil from burst heating systems. All this, together with sewage and other products of urban dwelling, was transported by the swirling currents.

The terrible mixture was swept at high speed through most of the city, penetrating everything in its path. Contents of shops and homes were permeated with this sludge. The flood waters rose to engulf statues and paintings hanging on walls in galleries, churches, museums and private dwellings. The torrential waters poured against the great beam-barred doors of churches, finally smashing them aside. The greatest single loss to art occurred at the Church of Santa Croce where Giovanni Cimabue's 'Crucific' was damaged beyond repair.

At dawn a lightening sky revealed the city in a state of devastation. The flood had engulfed 7,500 acres of land. In some places the water had reached fourteen feet above street level. From an aircraft, Florence resembled nearby Venice, without the benefit of bridges. Everywhere people were stranded in upper floors or on roofs.

The city's great collections were partially submerged. In only a few cases were curators alerted in time to attempt a rescue of priceless objects and documents. Among those summoned were Professor Ugo Procacci, Superintendent of Fine Arts, and Doctor Umberto Baldini, Director of Restoration, at the Uffizi Gallery. They struggled waist deep in water to remove threatened paintings from the museum passageways extending along the Ponte Vecchio. To the courageous efforts of a few people in those early hours we owe thanks for the salvage of many important works. They braved the flood, disregarding their own safety, homes and possessions in their concern for works entrusted to their care and prized by scholars and art lovers the world over.

Similar scenes of chaos occurred throughout the city. Flood waters surged through the archeological museum, smashing nearly the whole collection. In the days following, the director likened it to an archeological excavation site. Broken pots and artifacts were buried beneath layers of silt which would have to be sieved. The catalogues of the collection were fortunately saved but many items are irreparable.

As news of the plight of Florence was broadcast to the world immediate action was taken by many agencies and individuals. For those outside of Florence it was impossible to assess accurately the extent of destruction to works of art. People, in their eagerness to act, made mistakes. A group of restorers from the United States flew immediately to Florence, only to find there was nothing ready to be restored. Rescue operations requiring physical strength and stamina were initially the most valuable contribution.

Water-soaked books and bindings awaiting restoration

Restorers working on a large flood-soaked panel painting in Florence

The actual work of restoration would come later; the need now was for first aid. To this challenge the much maligned students arose and were credited for the major recovery of works of art in the race against time and decay.

As the flood waters rose, the lower portions of paintings hanging on gallery and church walls were permeated with mud and oil. Capillary action caused further damage to areas above the water line. Initially the paint held on most canvases and panels when the water swept through. In those cases when it did not, fragments were washed away and lost for ever. As the flood water subsided, the paint films began to buckle and flake. This was a moment of extreme urgency. Under the guidance of restorers, teams of art students and others collected together what fragments of paint could be found. These were placed in polythene envelopes to accompany the paintings. The paintings were faced with small sheets of mulberry tissue adhered by coats of paraloid B-72.

Nystatin, an antibiotic, was sprayed on paintings to arrest mould growth.

The majority of the paintings were on large, ponderous panels which needed to be kept damp and under supervised humidity control as rapid drying would be disastrous to the wood and paint. These were transported to the ancient Limonaia, a winter shelter for lemon trees at the Pitti Palace.

At the National Library hundreds of students formed human chains to pass the soggy volumes up from the mire. Often gas masks were worn to lessen the stench of rotting leather bindings and sewage. Over a million volumes were recovered in three weeks of continual labour. The saturated books, documents and works of art on paper were a terrible sight. Ornate gilt leather bindings were reduced to shrunken pulp.

Apart from books and paintings, countless treasured relics were involved in the flood, including statues, furniture, armour, tapestries and all manner of art objects. They would require the attention of specialists from each branch of restoration.

A great debt of gratitude is owed to the army of students from many lands who, in their desire to be of assistance, worked unceasingly under the most trying conditions in those early days. The human need was equally great. Many students aided the citizens of Florence in cleaning away the debris from streets, homes and shops. It would have been a pity had human suffering been overlooked in order that art treasures might be saved, but in the end both humanity and art were served.

Aftermath

In July 1967, eight months after the flood, I had the honour of joining the British restoring team in Florence, under the auspices of the Italian Art and Archives Rescue Fund. We worked under expert leadership within the walls of the Fortessa da Basso, designed by Michelangelo. In what was perhaps the most remarkable feat of restoration, these old barracks had been renovated and transformed into a superb restoration laboratory within a few short months. Equipment and materials were donated by many countries. The impressive array included an abundance of binocular microscopes, retouching lamps, easels and lining tables.

The panel paintings had been moved from the Limonaia to the laboratory. The vast length of the Fortessa barracks was filled with large tables and sawhorses supporting panel paintings. Many of the paint surfaces gave the impression of a three-dimensional museum diorama illustrating a storm at sea. Buckled paint layers were forced upwards in rippling waves, a sight to dismay even the most experienced restorer. Many of these pictures were designated for transfer to new supports.

The large sums of money for equipment and maintenance of the restorers in Florence were raised by each participating country. Art museums, clubs, institutional and private galleries arranged special benefit exhibitions with the proceeds donated to Florentine relief. The largest fund was raised in America and administered under the title Committee for the Rescue of Italian Art, known as CRIA. They contributed large sums to the restoration of the panel paintings and library archives in particular. In Great Britain, the funds contributed were administered under the title The Italian Art and Archives Rescue Fund.

In certain aspects the flood may prove of some benefit to the future existence of works of antiquity. It has underlined the need for sensible storage of works of art. Officials must try to evolve plans to safeguard their collections against all possible disasters. Basements are not particularly suitable places to store valuable works, as the Florentine flood proved.

As a result of the flood, more has been done to enlighten the public about the valuable work of restorers than all the cleaned paintings exhibited in museums. The need to establish more training centres for art conservation has been shown. It has provided an impetus for the Italian art administration to increase their own limited training programmes. Young Italian aspirants have been able to work alongside restorers from all over the world. The centres now established in Florence have a long future, in so far as unfinished work is concerned. Time estimates on the flood-damaged works vary from ten to twenty years for completion.

Meanwhile, countless works in other collections will need attention in the natural course of ageing. More centres are needed where students may be able to further the knowledge they gained while treating art and historical objects after the flood. There will be no need to look far for materials to use in class demonstrations.

BIBLIOGRAPHICAL NOTES

The number of published books available which deal solely with the subject of restoration is limited. Many have become obsolete in the light of modern restoring techniques and scientific advancements. The main sources of information pertaining to current research in the field of restoration are contained in a few technical journals and published conference seminar papers.

Many books deal only partially with restoration. A short chapter may be incorporated as relevant to detailed information on art history or technique. Few books have been written by restorers on the subject.

The bibliography is devoted principally to authoritative publications which relate to material described in this book. They are listed under separate subject headings with a brief description of the contents of each text. Several out-of-print books have been republished by Dover Publications Inc of New York as inexpensive paperbacks.

A few of the more important early manuscripts instructing on art techniques, recipes and theory are included for their reference value.

Restoring and Preservation

Bradley, Morton C. *The Treatment of Pictures*. Art Technology, Cambridge, Mass, 1950.

Published in the form of a loose-leaf notebook for future additions. Bradley is unsurpassed for step by step instructions in restoring procedures.

Clark, Carl D. *Pictures, their Preservation and Restoration*. The Standard Arts Press, Butler, Maryland, 1959.

An interesting book with many photographs. Several restoring processes are illustrated in photographic sequence. There are numerous formulas given and an extensive chapter is devoted to the restoration and preservation of old photographs.

Keck, Caroline K. *A Handbook on the Care of Paintings*. American Association for State and Local History, Nashville, Tennessee, 1965.

This small book is oriented towards the curators of historical agencies and small museums. It is written clearly and contains information of value to restorers and artists alike.

Keck, Caroline K. *How to Take Care of your Pictures*. Museum of Modern Art and Brooklyn Museum, New York, 1954.

A brief practical guide for the collector with descriptions of a few restoring techniques.

Mills, John FitzMaurice. *Picture Cleaning and Restoration*. Winsor & Newton Limited, London.

A useful booklet on the preservation and care of pictures.

Pettenkofer, Max V. *On Oil Painting and Conservation for Picture Galleries by Means of the Regeneration Process*. (Published in the German language.) Braunschweig, 1870.

A description and manifesto of the patented Pettenkofer Regeneration Method, by which he claimed it would be unnecessary to remove old varnish from pictures in the future.

Plenderleith, H. J. *The Conservation of Antiquities and Works of Art. Treatment, Repair and Restoration*. Oxford University Press, London, 1956.

A scholarly examination of the problems and treatment of museum and cultural properties. The art objects and artifacts examined include paper, paintings, metal, stone, bone, leather and pottery.

Stout, George L. *The Care of Pictures*. Columbia University Press, New York, 1948.

This small book is something of a classic on the subject. It is well constructed and easily comprehended. The text encompasses a wider range than the title implies. It is most valuable for describing the examination of a painting's structure and the causes and effects of deterioration. A reprinting of the book is well deserved.

An Exhibition of Cleaned Pictures. Printed for the Trustees of the National Gallery, London.

The published catalogue of the exhibition held at the National Gallery in 1947. The condition and treatment of the individual pictures cleaned between 1936 and 1947 are described. The inclusion of a catalogue in this bibliography is justified by the controversy the exhibition raised.

Artists' Techniques and Materials

Cennini, Cennino d'Andrea. *The Craftsman's Handbook.* Yale University Press, 1933. Republished by Dover.

An English translation by D. V. Thompson of Yale University Press's *Il Libro dell' Arte* published in 1933.

The·famous early fifteenth century Florentine treatise on medieval painting which has been responsible for revealing many secret recipes and techniques. Without this documentation they might have been lost for ever.

Constable, W. G. *The Painters' Workshop.* Oxford University Press, London, 1954.

A most interesting and informative book on the established working procedures of the Old Masters' studios and guilds. One chapter is given to describing the deterioration, preservation and repair of pictures.

Doerner, Max. *The Materials of the Artist and their Use in Painting.* First published in German. Munich, 1922. Most recent revised edition, Harrap, London, 1955.

A book long established as invaluable for the artist. It is comprehensive in its examination of artists' techniques and materials. A chapter is devoted to restoring easel pictures. Some of the restoring methods described are no longer practised but they are of interest.

Eastlake, C. L. *The Methods and Materials of Painting of the Great Schools and Masters.* Republished in two volumes by Dover, 1960.

The first volume of this book was published in 1847 and the second volume in 1869. It was then entitled *Materials for a History of Oil Painting.* Charles Eastlake was a director of the National Gallery, London. He was a renowned scholar, extracting most of the pertinent facts on the methods and materials of the past from archive sources extending from early antiquity.

Greek, Roman and Medieval techniques are accurately described. The descriptions of the painting methods of Leonardo, Raphael, Van Eyck and other artists were compiled from years of manuscript research in several languages.

Gettens, Rutherford, J. and Stout, George L. *Painting Materials: A Short*

Encyclopaedia. First published, D. Van Nostrand, New York, 1942. Republished by Dover, 1966.

One of the most authoritative books on the subject of painting materials. The text is factual and timeless.

Herberts, Kurt Dr. *The Complete Book of Artists' Techniques.* Thames & Hudson, London, 1958. Translated from the German *Die Mal Techniken.*

This book is divided into three principal sections and an appendix. It is visually handsome and explores an extensive list of techniques used by artists from rock and wall paintings to painting on ivory and porcelain.

Hiler, Hilaire. *The Painter's Pocketbook of Methods and Materials.* Faber & Faber, London, 1937. Reprinted 1964.

A small book containing useful information for the painter. It is concise and easily read.

Hours, Madeleine. *Secrets of the Great Masters.* Laffont, Paris, 1964. Published in English by Hamlyn, Feltham, Middlesex.

The book evolved from a series of lectures given on French television. Interesting laboratory discoveries made with the aid of scientific apparatus are related. The book was awarded a prize as the finest illustrated publication in France.

Lamb, Lynton. *Materials and Methods of Painting.* Oxford University Press, London, 1970.

A small handbook for artists with photographic illustrations. Contemporary media and techniques are described.

Laurie, A. P. *The Painter's Methods and Materials.* London, 1926. Republished by Dover, 1967.

A scholarly book containing much useful information for the artist and restorer. Investigations are made into pigments, oils, varnishes and supports. A chapter is given to the preservation and cleaning of pictures. This is mainly of interest with regard to restoring methods of the period.

Laurie, A. P. *The Pigments and Mediums of the Old Masters.* Macmillan, London, 1914.

The examination of pigments and mediums of the Old Masters by scientific means. Microscopic examination and tests for chemical reactions are described with clarity. A special chapter is devoted to the micro-photographic study of brushwork.

Laurie, A. P. *The Technique of the Great Painters*. Caroll & Nicholson, London, 1949.

The text includes an interesting section on the building up of a painting in the fourteenth and fifteenth centuries. Medieval pigments and varnishes are described as well as painting with yolk of egg, emulsions and mediums .

Maroger, Jacques. *The Secret Formulas and Techniques of the Masters*. Studio Publications, New York, 1948. Translated from the French.

The book is written by a former technical director of the Laboratory of the Louvre Museum and president of the Restorers of France. As the title suggests, the book explores the working methods and recipes of the great painters. There is the inevitable probing of the Van Eyck technique with some interesting insights.

Massey, Robert. *Formulas for Artists*. Batsford, London, 1968.

Over 200 Renaissance to modern laboratory-tested recipes carried out by the author.

Mayer, Ralph. *The Artist's Handbook of Materials and Techniques*. New York, 1938. Recent revised edition, Faber, London, 1965.

One of the most popular books of its kind. It has enjoyed a wide circulation and may be found on the bookshelves of most professional artists and restorers. A comprehensive chapter on the conservation of pictures is included.

Mayer, Ralph. *The Painter's Craft*. D. Van Nostrand, New York, 1966.

A practical book of modern painting materials and studio equipment with several instructive photographs.

Merrifield, Mary P. *Original Treatises, dating from the Twelfth to the Eighteenth Centuries, on the Arts of Painting*. John Murray, London, 1849.

The writing is contained in two volumes. Mrs Merrifield discourses on the history of the techniques of paintings with facts derived from various early manuscripts. A section on restoring translated from Italian sources is historically enlightening.

Thompson, Daniel V. *The Materials and Techniques of Medieval Painting*. Originally published by Constable, 1936. Republished by Dover, 1956.

An authoritative text based on many years of experience in the analysis of medieval paintings and medieval manuscripts.

Thompson, Daniel V. *The Practice of Tempera Painting*. First published by Yale University Press, 1936. Republished by Dover, 1962.

The author explains the essentials of tempera painting with the authority of many years' research into medieval and Renaissance manuscripts.

Vasari, G. *Vasari on Technique*. Florence, 1550. (Translated by L. S. Macklehouse) London, 1907. Republished by Dover, 1960.

This book is by the outstanding biographer of the Renaissance artists. It is an introduction to the arts of architecture, sculpture and painting. It preceded his work *The Lives of the Most Eminent Italian Architects, Painters and Sculptors*.

Scientific Aspects

Burroughs, Alan. *Art Criticism from a Laboratory*. Little Brown & Co, Boston, 1938.

A description of the techniques and interpretation of X-rays used for examining paintings.

Church, A. H. *The Chemistry of Paints and Painting*. Seeley Service, London, 1915.

In spite of the date of publication, this book still has useful information to impart. It is concerned with the chemical properties of painting materials. The chapters pertaining to restoration and preservation are relevant to our attitudes today.

de Wild, A. M. *The Scientific Examination of Pictures*. G. Bell, London, 1929.

The investigation and documentation of microscopic paint samples from many original Dutch and Flemish paintings. Tables and graphs are used to illustrate the text. A chapter is devoted to the restoration and conservation of paintings.

Harley, R. D. *Artist's Pigments c* 1600-1835. Butterworth, London, 1970.

Based on little known English documentary sources, this book is a revised version of a doctorial thesis. It brings to light many interesting aspects in the composition and development of pigments.

Martin, J. H. and Morgans, W. M. *Guide to Pigments and to Varnish and Lacquer Constituents*. Leonard Hill, London, 1954.

An alphabetically arranged book useful for quick reference. Brief descriptions and chemical formulas are provided.

Rawlins, F. I. G. *From the National Gallery Laboratory*.

Printed for the Trustees of the National Gallery, London, 1940.

The text and illustrations pertain to pictures in the National Gallery collection. There are many interesting X-rays, infra-red photographs and photomicrographs.

Paper and Prints

Barrow, William J. *Manuscripts and Documents: their Deterioration and Restoration.* University of Virginia Press, Charlottesville, 1955.

A text by the inventor of the Barrow lamination process.

Barrow, William J. *Procedures and Equipment used in the Barrow Method of Restoring Manuscripts and Documents.* The State Library Building, Richmond, Virginia, 1950.

A useful text for libraries and paper conservation laboratories.

Gaehde, C. M. and Zigrosser, C. *A Guide to the Collecting and Care of Original Prints.* Crown, New York, 1965.

This is an introduction to prints and collecting by the Vice President of the Print Council of America, with an expert restorer contributing a chapter on the care and conservation of fine prints.

Green, J. Barcham. *Paper Making by Hand in* 1967. Maidstone, England, 1967.

An illustrated booklet explaining the processes involved in the manufacture of handmade papers.

Gross, Anthony. *Etching, Engraving and Intaglio Printing.* Oxford University Press, London, 1970.

A long-awaited book by the British etching master, Anthony Gross. Particularly interesting reading for its many anecdotes and personal reflections on the historical and modern aspects of etching techniques.

Hind, Arthur M. *A History of Engraving and Etching.* Republished by Dover, 1963.

A fine reference book by Mr Hind, a former keeper of prints and drawings at the British Museum. The book lists and classifies the important etchers and engravers from the fifteenth century to the year 1914. The various printing processes are described in detail.

Labarre, D. J. *Dictionary and Encyclopaedia of Paper and Paper Making.* Swets & Zeitlinger, Amsterdam, 1962.

A comprehensive work valuable to anyone interested in the process of papermaking.

Lumsden, E. S. *The Art of Etching*. Seeley Service, London, 1924. Republished by Dover, 1962.

The technique of etching and engraving is described in detail. The history of etching is related with emphasis on the great masters, Durer, Rembrandt, Goya, Whistler, etc. Numerous brief biographies of nineteenth-century British masters and modern etchers.

Restoration and Preservation of Library Resources, Documents and Books. Translated from the Russian. Distributed by Oldbourne Press, London.

The restoration techniques of libraries and laboratories in the Soviet Union are described. The means of controlling insects and mould fungi are presented in detail.

Forgery

Arnau, Frank. *Three Thousand Years of Deception in Art and Antiques*. Cape, London, 1961. Translated from the German.

As the title suggests, the book is a comprehensive survey of known forgeries over the centuries.

Kilbracken, John R. G., Baron. *Van Meegeren: A Case History*. Nelson, London, 1967.

The life story of Han Van Meegeren.

Kurz, Otto. *Fakes*. Faber & Faber, London, 1948. Republished by Dover, 1967. (Revised and enlarged.)

A wide range of fakes is described in various arts including architecture, painting, prints, glass, metal, ceramics, furniture, tapestry, etc.

Mendax, Fritz. *Art Fakes and Forgeries*. Laurie, London, 1955. Translated from the German.

A compilation of forgeries throughout history. The subjects include Durer, Van Meegeren, and Otto Wacker's faked Van Gogh paintings.

Schuller, Sepp. *Forgers, Dealers, Experts*. Barker, London, 1959. Translated from the German.

Written with the German reader in mind; it contains interesting stories and anecdotes about forged paintings, sculpture and furniture.

Synthetic Media

Duca, Alfred. *Polymer Tempera Handbook*. Polymer Tempera Inc, Somerville, Mass, 1956.
The manufacture and technique of painting with polymer tempera paints.

Jensen, Lawrence N. *Synthetic Painting Media*. Prentice-Hall, Englewood Cliffs, New Jersey, 1964.
This book is one of the first to explore in depth the new world of synthetic media for the fine arts. A summary of traditional media is included in the text for comparison.

Mills, John FitzMaurice. *Acrylic Painting*. Pitman, London, 1965.
An account of the technique of using acrylic paints, written with clarity for the uninitiated.

Woody, Russell O. *Painting with Synthetic Media*. Reinhold, New York, 1965.
A survey of synthetic media. Contemporary painters will find the book most instructive.

Selective Reading

Batini, Giorgio. *4 November 1966: The River Arno in the Museums of Florence*. Bonechi, Florence, 1967.
An assessment of the flood damage to documents and works of art in the museums of Florence.

Meiss, Millard. *The Great Age of Fresco: Discoveries, Recoveries and Survivals*. Phaidon, London, 1970.
A large profusely illustrated book presenting the technique of fresco painting, together with historical notes. The method of detaching frescoes and their preservation are examined in depth.

Pars, H. H. *Pictures in Peril*. Faber, London, 1957. Translated from the German *Noch Leuchten Die Bilder*.
A diverse publication tracing the history of paintings stolen, mutilated, burnt or badly cared for and pictures subjected to the ravages and pillage of war. A chapter is devoted to restoration.

Toch, Maximilian. *Paints, Paintings and Restoration*. D. Van Nostrand, New York, 1931. Second edition, 1945.

A small book discoursing on pigments, solvents, varnishes, photography and imitations with a short chapter on restoring.

Edited. *Frescoes from Florence*. Arts Council of Great Britain, London, 1969.

The catalogue of the exhibition of detached Florentine frescoes shown in London at the Hayward Gallery. It is profusely illustrated and contains a detailed account of the technique of frescoes together with their removal and transfer.

Early Manuscripts and Writings

De Mayerne, Theodore, Baron. *Sloane 2052*, About 1620.

An important treatise on art techniques of the time. Theophilus.

Diversarum Artium Schedula. Edited by R. Hendrie, 1947.

A twelfth-century text on art and technique.

The Strasburg Manuscript. A Medieval Painter's Handbook. Tiranti, London, 1966.

This publication is a translation by Viola and Rosamund Borradaile of the old German text. The manuscript is an early source of German painting methods. It is an instructional book with northern recipes and techniques for painting and illumination.

Journals and Periodicals

The Burlington Magazine. Published monthly by Burlington Magazines, London.

A magazine devoted to fine art and antiques. It occasionally publishes scholarly articles concerning restoration.

Museums Journal. Published by the Museums Association, London.

A magazine of broad scope with articles relating to every aspect of museum administration, display, conservation, etc.

Studies in Conservation. Published quarterly by the International Institute for the Conservation of Historic and Artistic Works, London.

A publication devoted to the furtherance of the principles of conservation. Articles on the scientific aspects of restoring are predominant. This publication replaces *Technical Studies in the Field of Fine Arts*.

INDEX

ACKNOWLEDGEMENTS

I wish to acknowledge my appreciation for the assistance given me by Mr Stavros Mihalarias, Mr Ben Johnson and Mr and Mrs Adam Raft, who provided photographs used for this book. I am indebted to Mr David Stein, Arthur Barker Ltd, Sotheby & Co and Winsor & Newton Ltd for their kind permission in allowing me to quote from their original sources.

I wish to thank my friends in the restoring profession who have remained tolerant and exceedingly generous with their time and knowledge.

I owe a special debt of gratitude to Mr Edward H. Spiro-Cookridge, whose friendship, encouragement and advice were instrumental in my undertaking the writing of this book. Lastly I wish to acknowledge the indispensable contribution of Mrs Patricia Kelly, who helped to type, edit and revise this manuscript. For her careful, competent, dedicated perseverance I am deeply grateful.